CAMBRIDGE ENGLISH
for schools
Workbook Three

ANDREW LITTLEJOHN & DIANA HICKS

CAMBRIDGE
UNIVERSITY PRESS

PUBLISHED BY THE PRESS SYNDICATE OF THE UNIVERSITY OF CAMBRIDGE
The Pitt Building, Trumpington Street, Cambridge CB2 1RP, United Kingdom

CAMBRIDGE UNIVERSITY PRESS
The Edinburgh Building, Cambridge CB2 2RU, United Kingdom
40 West 20th Street, New York, NY 10011-4211, USA
10 Stamford Road, Oakleigh, Melbourne 3166, Australia

First published 1997
Reprinted 1998

Printed in the United Kingdom at the University Press, Cambridge.

ISBN 0 521 42175 6 Workbook
ISBN 0 521 42171 3 Student's Book
ISBN 0 521 42179 9 Teacher's Book
ISBN 0 521 42128 4 Class Cassette Set
ISBN 0 521 42132 2 Workbook Cassette

Contents

Memories; getting
ready to learn English;
Your Language
Record

1 *Reading and*
writing

2 *Preparation for*
learning

3 *Your Language*
Record

1 Moving on

1 Looking back

1.1 The first time

Think about the first time you did something
or received something. For example:

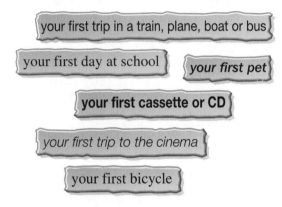

your first trip in a train, plane, boat or bus

your first day at school   *your first pet*

your first cassette or CD

your first trip to the cinema

your first bicycle

Choose a topic and make some notes.

Write a short paragraph about it.

I can remember the first … I was … years
old. My friends …

Read through what you wrote and check your
spelling, grammar and vocabulary.

Next lesson, you can compare memories with
other students in your class.

1.2 Some memories

Here are some descriptions written by other
people. What are they describing, do you
think?

1… It was a very big room, with very high
ceilings. I sat at a desk near the window,
but I couldn't see anything because the
windows were too high. There was a
large map of the world on the wall and
an old blackboard. I don't think I was
worried or frightened. There was a boy
next to me and he was crying and
crying. He didn't want to stay there …

2… It was fantastic! We were really high
up, and you could see everything. All the
houses and people below looked really small.
It was very quiet as well — but cold! The
wind was blowing a little bit and we moved
very slowly. Every few minutes, the pilot
turned the fire on to keep us up in the
air. There were about eight of us in the
basket. I think we were in the air about
an hour. I wish I could do it again!

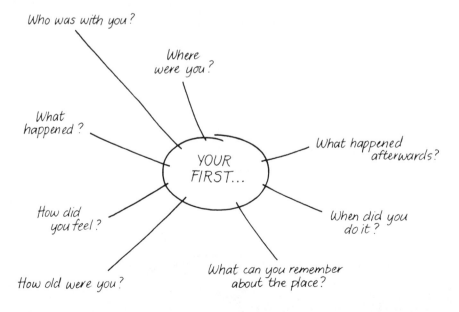

Who was with you?

Where
were you?

What
happened?

What happened
afterwards?

YOUR
FIRST…

How did
you feel?

When did you
do it?

How old were you?

What can you remember
about the place?

2 Getting ready to learn

2.1 Classroom questions

Can you match the questions with the situations?

1	You can't hear the cassette.	a	Can you speak more slowly, please?
2	You haven't got a pencil.	b	Please can you check this exercise?
3	Someone is speaking too fast.	c	I'm sorry. I don't understand.
4	You don't understand.	d	Can you tell me what … means?
5	You can't spell something.	e	Can you turn the volume up, please?
6	You don't know the word in English.	f	Has anyone got a pen or a pencil?
7	You can't pronounce a word.	g	I'm sorry. I didn't hear what you said.
8	You don't know what a word means.	h	What's the English word for …?
9	You can't hear what the teacher says.	i	How do you write that word?
10	You have finished the exercise.	j	How do you pronounce this word?

2.2 The things you need

Look at the picture and find eight things in the word puzzle that you need to help you learn.

```
C A S S E T T E P L A Y E R Y
D J K H K U H E N Q L A F D F
I C A S S E T T E U W O Q E F
C P O I Y G R A M M A R A G H
T P E N C I L Q U A Y H S M N
I V C D S A W Q W E R Y U U I
O H U I W O R K B O O K F P L
N H Y E G C R U B B E R C W Q
A J U E H J Q S A Z C V G D S
R L A N G U A G E R E C O R D
Y H Y E G W H U Q L P O W N B
```

3 Your Language Record

Your new language record has three sections. Where would you put these things? Write them in the correct list. (Look in your Student's Book, Unit 1 Exercise 4.)

the names of types of furniture
notes about the Present simple
the words from Unit 1
some useful phrases for shopping
different words to describe people
notes about the Past simple
how to offer people something

Record of Language Use

....

....

....

Word Groups

....

....

....

Grammar Record

....

....

....

2 The living museum

**Look at the Test in Unit 2 and
Supplementary Unit B in your
Student's Book. Do you need more
practice? Choose the parts that you
need to do.**

1 In the sports room

1.1 What's in the gym?

Mark is reading the descriptions of the
equipment in the gym. Can you match the
descriptions with the equipment?

1
> This machine helps your heart beat quickly.
> Put your feet carefully on the pedals. Ride
> slowly for one minute, then increase speed
> gradually. Stop after five minutes.

2
> Sit comfortably on the seat – you can move it
> to the correct position. Hold the oars tightly
> and push your arms firmly. Row continuously
> for four minutes.

3
> Stand near the front of the machine and
> move the dial to 1. Start jogging very gently
> for 45 seconds, move the dial to 2 and start
> jogging more quickly for another 45 seconds.
> Increase the speed to 5 and run fast for two
> minutes.

4
> Weights are dangerous! We check this
> machine frequently but check it carefully
> yourself before you start! Don't use heavy
> weights immediately! Start gradually. Put the
> weights very carefully on the bottom of the
> machine. Push hard with your legs 20 times.

5
> Sit back comfortably on the bench. Put your
> arms firmly around the two parts of the
> machine. Pull your arms together gradually.
> Repeat 15 times. If the weight is too heavy,
> stop immediately.

1.2 Different adverbs

Now find the adverbs in the descriptions and
the rules. Write the adverbs with 'ly' in circle
A and the adverbs without 'ly' in circle B.

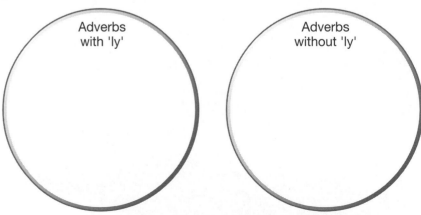

Adverbs
with 'ly'

Adverbs
without 'ly'

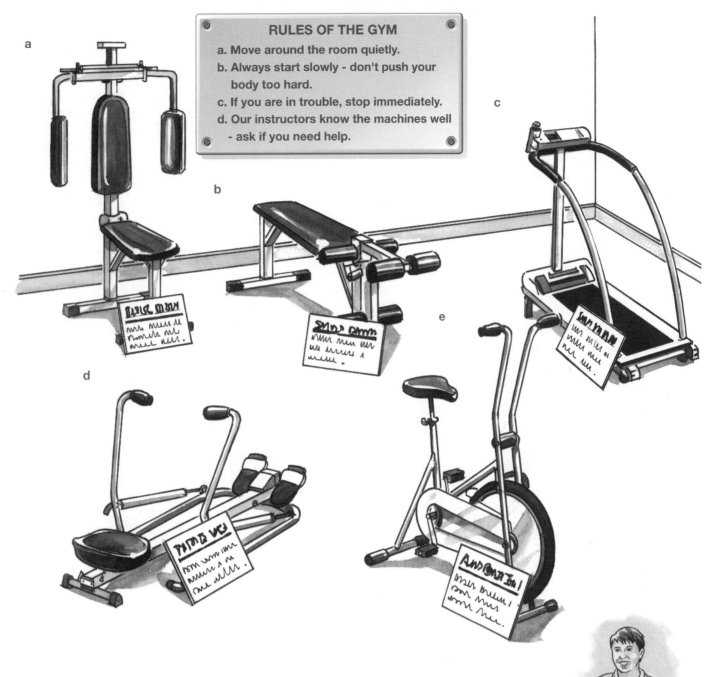

RULES OF THE GYM

a. Move around the room quietly.
b. Always start slowly - don't push your body too hard.
c. If you are in trouble, stop immediately.
d. Our instructors know the machines well - ask if you need help.

1.3 An exercise programme

Mark is talking to Steve Johnson, an exercise trainer, about the equipment in the gym. Use the verbs in brackets to complete the sentences.

MARK: Do you use all the machines every day, Steve?

STEVE: No, not all of them!

MARK: Which ones do you like best?

STEVE: Well, I love _____ (run) so I use the jogging machine every day.

MARK: And what about the boat?

STEVE: Well, I enjoy _____ (row) against machines! When I first started _____ (use) it I was on level 3 but now I'm on level 7.

MARK: What about the cycle machine?

STEVE: I don't mind _____ (cycle). My legs are quite strong because I run every day.

MARK: When did you begin _____ (train)?

STEVE: About a year ago. I hated _____ (work) in an office.

MARK: So, what part of this job do you like best?

STEVE: I like _____ (be) able to use all the equipment. Why don't you try?

MARK: OK … but not today!

2 In the rainforest room

Read about how the continents moved. Can you write the correct form of the verb in the spaces?

Gondwanaland and the rainforests of New Guinea

notice

In 1869, Alfred Wallace, a scientist, [1]_____ that the plants and animals in the south and the north of New

discover

Guinea are very different. He also [2]_____ that many plants and animals in the south are similar to plants and animals in Australia. He said that there was a 'line' that went through south Asia, with different animals and plants

call

on each side of the line. He [3]_____ this 'Wallace's line'.

move

How did this happen? Today, scientists think that millions of years ago, all the land [4]_____ together and

form

[5]_____ one big continent, 'Pangaea' (Greek for 'all land').

divide

Later Pangaea [6]_____ into two supercontinents –
Gondwanaland and Laurasia. These two supercontinents

separate

then [7]_____ into smaller pieces. Part of Gondwanaland

move   crash

[8]_____ north and [9]_____ into part of Laurasia. The south of New Guinea was part of Gondwanaland and the north

crash

of New Guinea was part of Laurasia. When they [10]_____

push

together, they [11]_____ the land up – to make mountains.

stay

The animals and plants from Gondwanaland [12]_____ on one side of the mountains and the animals and plants from

stay

Laurasia [13]_____ on the other side. So that's why, today, they are different.

continue

Gondwanaland and Laurasia [14]_____ to move and break up. Today we have Africa, South America, Australia, Antarctica, India and southern Asia from Gondwanaland, and North America, Europe and northern Asia from Laurasia.

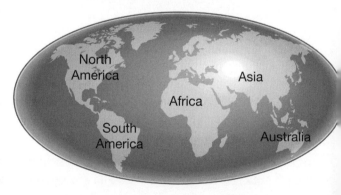

3 In the past discoveries room

3.1 The pyramid city

Read about Teotihuacan, an ancient city in Mexico.

The city of Teotihuacan, near Mexico City, is about 2,000 years old. For 700 years, it was the largest city in the world – over 200,000 people lived there in 500 AD. Then, around 750 AD, the people left the city. No one knows for certain why they left the city. Archaeological work began in Teotihuacan in 1918 and we now know a lot about life there. It took 200 years to build the main pyramid. Inside the pyramid, archaeologists found many things which gave them clues about life in the city.

We know that the 'Teotihuacanos' understood the movement of the stars. We also know that they ate different kinds of meat and they caught fish. They drank 'pulque' – a special drink that they made from plants. In the market they bought and sold things. We don't know what language they spoke or if they knew how to write.

3.2 Irregular verbs

Look back at the text. There are 16 irregular past tense verbs. Can you find them? Write them around the word square and then try to find the infinitive.

....

was

```
A  H  B  E  H  U  W  D  R  I  N  K  H
F  G  I  V  E  B  N  H  F  R  W  S  E
I  J  I  S  P  E  A  K  L  P  W  W  A          left
N  D  S  A  D  Q  W  L  E  A  V  E  T
D  J  A  X  K  N  O  W  H  Q  P  K  T
B  U  Y  L  J  O  P  M  A  K  E  G  A
B  E  G  I  N  W  J  W  R  I  T  E  K
K  O  U  N  D  E  R  S  T  A  N  D  E
C  A  T  C  H  T  K  O  S  E  L  L  A
```

began

3.3 Who is right?

In the past discoveries room Mark met his younger friend, Ben. They talked about life in Teotihuacan. Can you complete Mark's answers?

BEN: Hi, Mark. What did you think of the Teotihuacan exhibition?

MARK: Fantastic! But it didn't tell us about what they did in their free time.

BEN: Do you think they had television?

MARK: No, *they didn't have television* 1,500 years ago, Ben!

BEN: Maybe they went to the cinema?

MARK: Cinema! They .... then.

BEN: Do you think they listened to the radio?

MARK: ....

BEN: Well, perhaps the children rode bicycles.

MARK: ....

BEN: Perhaps they played on their computers.

MARK: ....

BEN: Well, what a boring life they had!

3.4 More questions

Can you write some more questions about Teotihuacan? Here are some ideas.

How did they build the pyramids? Why did they build them? Why did they leave the city? Where did they go?

clothes? travel? medicine? school? food? free time? science?

THEME A

Vocabulary; Past
continuous; /ə/, /ɒ/;
speaking; reading;
Scott and
Amundsen

1 *Vocabulary*

2 *Past continuous*

3 *any …*

4 */ə/, /ɒ/*

5 *Reading; Past
continuous*

FOCUS ON 3
Exploration
Topic and language

1 What's the word?

Can you write the correct word in the puzzle?
Many of them are in Exercise 8 in your
Student's Book.

1 When ice gets warm, it begins to
....

2 To look for something very carefully.

3 The enormous ocean that Magellan sailed
across.

4 Franklin was looking for a ....
through the Arctic.

5 The people who live in the Arctic.

6 The .... of Spain sent Magellan
to the Spice Islands.

7 Magellan's ships were the first ships to
.... around the world.

8 A short message.

9 Thor Heyerdahl was a Norwegian
....

10 Britain is in the continent of ....

11 In 1494, Spain and Portugal agreed to
.... the non-Christian world
between them.

12 Heyerdahl thought that the ancient Egyptians
sailed across the .... to America.

13 The first people in Australia.

2 What were they doing?

On July 26th, 1845, some sailors saw
Franklin's ships when they were entering the
bay. What were the other sailors doing? Look
at the picture and write a sentence about each
person. For example:

a *They were checking the fishing nets.*

3 Any way you want

Choose the correct word or words to complete each sentence.

any way   anywhere   anything   any time   anyone

1 Tomorrow is a holiday so I can get up at .... I like.
2 'What do you want for dinner?' '..! I eat everything.'
3 .... you go in the world you can find people that speak English.
4 The last time .... saw Franklin was in July 1846.
5 You can cook potatoes .... you want. You can fry them, roast them, boil them and bake them.

4 Say it clearly

Listen and say these sentences.

> Where **were** /wə/ you last night?
> I was watching / wɒt∫ɪŋ / television.

Listen and say /ə/ clearly.

> w**e**re   December   yest**er**day   nev**er**
> I have **a** cat   How **are** you?   Where w**ere** you last Septemb**er**?

Now listen and say /ɒ/ clearly.

> w**a**s   w**a**sh   bec**au**se   **o**ff   **o**ffice   r**o**ck
> r**o**cket   w**a**tching
> He w**a**sn't in the **o**ffice today bec**au**se he was ill.

5 A race to the South Pole

5.1 Tragedy in Antarctica

The story of Captain Robert Scott in Antarctica is one of the saddest stories in the history of exploration. Read about what happened to Scott and his men.

A race to the South Pole – and tragedy

Captain Robert Scott wanted to be the first person to reach the South Pole. In 1911, he planned a trip to Antarctica, but while he was preparing to leave he heard about Roald Amundsen. Amundsen, from Norway, also wanted to be the first person to reach the South Pole. The race was on.

Scott started the trip on November 1st, 1911. With him, he had eleven men, ponies, dogs, snow tractors and sledges. They were going to cross nearly 3,000 kilometres of ice – the longest journey by sledge in history.

Problems in the ice

Very soon, Scott's expedition had terrible problems. The wind was blowing very hard and all the ponies died from the cold. Then, on December 31st, the snow tractors broke down and seven of the men had to go back. Scott and four other men continued across the ice. Scott didn't know it, but two weeks before that, on December 14th, Amundsen had already arrived at the South Pole – while Scott and his men were fighting their way across the ice.

At the South Pole

On January 18th, 1912, Scott finally reached the South Pole – when Amundsen was already sailing home. At the Pole, Scott found the Norwegian flag and a letter from Amundsen. Tired and weak, Scott and his men started their return journey, but while they were crossing the ice, one of the men fell and died. Another man died a few days later. The other three men tried to continue but the cold was too much for them. On March 29th, 1912, Scott and his men all died in the ice – only 18 kilometres from their camp.

Amundsen thought that the trip to the South Pole was going to make him famous. Instead, Scott became the hero.

5.2 What happened?

Look back at the story. Can you complete the list of events?

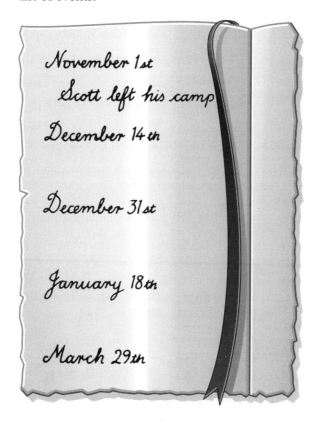

November 1st
Scott left his camp
December 14th

December 31st

January 18th

March 29th

5.3 What was happening?

What was happening when each of these things happened? Write a sentence about each one.

a Scott heard about Amundsen.

....

....

b The ponies died.

....

....

c Arnundsen arrived at the South Pole.

....

....

d Scott arrived at the South Pole.

....

....

e One of the men fell.

....

....

6 Talk to Lewis

Write your answers to Lewis' questions. Then talk to him on the cassette.

LEWIS: Hi there. How are you?

YOU: ....

LEWIS: I'm fine. Last night I was reading about the Franklin Expedition. It's a very sad story, isn't it?

YOU: ....

LEWIS: Where were they going when they disappeared?

YOU: ....

LEWIS: Oh yes, that's right. Franklin was an explorer, wasn't he? Do you know the names of any other explorers?

YOU: ....

....

....

....

LEWIS: What did they do?

YOU: ....

....

....

....

LEWIS: Oh yes, I think I've heard that before.

YOU: ....

LEWIS: Would you like to be an explorer?

YOU: ....

LEWIS: Why?

YOU: ....

....

....

....

LEWIS: Well, I don't think I want to be an explorer. It's too dangerous! I must go now. Talk to you later. Bye!

YOU: ....

Mysteries solved?
Topic and language

4

Zero conditional;
reading;
intonation:
falling tone; modal
verbs; writing and
speaking

1 *Zero conditional*

2 *Reading*

1 If and when

Can you match the two parts of each sentence?
Complete c and h with your own ideas.

1 If plants don't get water, …
2 If you don't wash, …
3 If you leave milk in the sun, …
4 If a car runs out of petrol, …
5 If you put water on a fire, …
6 When metal gets hot, …
7 When you are asleep, …
8 When rubber burns, …
9 When air gets hot, …
10 When air gets cold, …

a it goes out.
b it smells awful!
c ....
d it expands.
e they die.
f it falls.
g it rises.
h ....
i it goes bad.
j you smell.

2 The mysterious circles

2.1 In the wheat fields

Read about one of the strangest mysteries in England.

The mystery of the circles in the wheat fields

*Some years ago in Wiltshire, England, a farmer discovered
something very strange in one of his wheat fields – it was
an enormous circle, over 20 metres in diameter.*

Since then, many other circles have appeared
in the same area. They are all very similar.
The circles are perfect circles. Around them,
the wheat is completely vertical. Inside the circles,
the wheat is flat but not broken. It usually goes
anti-clockwise. Sometimes, there is another, bigger
circle around it where the wheat goes clockwise.
Dogs often refuse to go into the circles.

Many other strange things often happen near
the circles.

- Five circles appeared in a field after a man and
  a woman saw very bright lights in the sky.

- A farmer found white jelly in the centre of one
  circle. University scientists say they don't know
  what the jelly is.

- A pilot jumped from his plane in the area. The
  next day they found him – dead – near some
  circles.

- Two men waited all day and all night in the
  fields. They didn't see or hear anything
  unusual, but in the morning they found an
  enormous circle in front of them.

More circles appear every year, but more than
twenty years after the first circle, nobody has a
clear idea of where they come from.

3 *Falling tone*
4 *Modals*
5 *Writing and speaking*

2.2 What do you think?

Where do you think the circles come from? Here are some ideas. Tick (✓) two or three ideas that you think are possible causes. Put a cross against the ideas that you think are not the causes.

a   the wind

b   flying saucers from another planet

c   natural magnetic forces

d   people playing a trick

e   birds

f   rabbits or other small animals

g   the rain

h   cows or sheep

i   a helicopter

j   something else: ....

Read the text in Exercise 2.1 again and check your ideas. Next lesson compare with other students in your class.

2.3 What's the word?

Can you match each word to the correct diagram?

    vertical
    anti-clockwise
    circle
    clockwise
    diameter
    horizontal

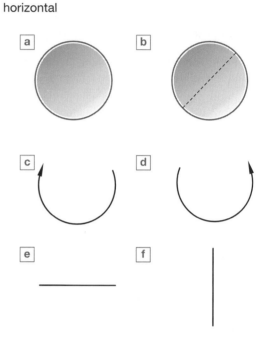

3   Say it clearly

3.1 Go down at the end!

 In English you usually go down at the end of sentences that are statements. Listen and say the sentences. Make your voice go

d
 o
  w
   n

If plants don't get water, they die. ➘

When metal gets hot, it expands. ➘

It's very cold today. ➘

She lives in the centre of town. ➘

Read these sentences. Make your voice go down at the end.

One of the greatest mysteries of all time is the *Marie Celeste*.

The *Hindenburg* was an airship that flew from Germany to France.

The Bermuda Triangle is an area in the Atlantic Ocean.

3.2 Up or down?

Listen to these sentences. Do they go up or down at the end? Draw an arrow for each one.

– ¹ Where do you live?

– ² I live in the city centre.

– ³ Is it far from here?

– ⁴ Yes, it's a long way. ⁵ Do you know where Central Park is?

– ⁶ Yes.

– ⁷ It's near there.

– ⁸ How do you come to school?

– ⁹ By bus.

Think! What type of sentences go UP? What type of sentences go DOWN? Check your answers at the end the Unit.

4 An exercise you should do

Choose one of these words for each gap.

don't have to   might   might   must   must   must   need   need
should   shouldn't

a Everyone .... wear a seat belt in a car. In some countries, it is the law and you .... wear a belt.

b You .... eat a lot of sweet things. It isn't good for you.

c You .... to eat well or you will be ill.

d In most countries, you .... pay taxes to the government.

e When you are an adult, you .... go to school.

f If you go to the south of England you .... see a circle in a wheat field.

g I .... go to the shops tomorrow because I .... to buy some things for school.

h It .... be sunny tomorrow.

5 Talk to Maggi

Find out about a mystery in your country and write your answers to Maggi's questions. Then talk to her on the cassette.

MAGGI: Hi there. How are you doing?
YOU: ....

MAGGI: At school, we're studying about mysteries at the moment. Can you tell me about a mystery in your country?
YOU: ....
....
....
....

MAGGI: That's interesting. Tell me more.
YOU: ....
....
....
....

MAGGI: When did this happen?
YOU: ....
....
....

MAGGI: Where exactly did this happen?
YOU: ....
....

MAGGI: That's fascinating. Do people know why this happened?
YOU: ....
....

MAGGI: What a good story! Thanks! I must go now. Bye!
YOU: ....
....

Answers to Exercise 3.2

1 down, 2 down, 3 up, 4 down, 5 up, 6 down, 7 down, 8 down, 9 down. Information questions (1, 8) and statements (2, 4, 6, 7, 9) go down. Yes/no questions (3, 5) go up.

Sounds to think
and write about

1 *Listening*

2 *Listening,
writing and
reading*

3 *Listening,
thinking and
writing*

5 Sounds to think about
Fluency

1 Where is it?

Listen to the cassette and look at the
pictures. Can you match the sounds to each
picture? Number the pictures 1–5.

a

In a cave

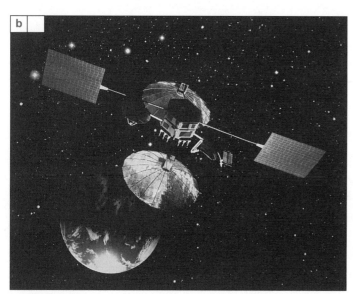

b

In space

c

In a forest

d

In Antarctica

e

At sea

2 In each place

2.1 Listen and think

🔲 Listen to each sound again and think. Imagine that you are in each place.

What is it like there? nice? horrible? frightening?
What can you see? people? animals? things?
How do you feel? afraid? happy? worried?

Make some notes about each place.

In Antarctica: wind, large open space, everything is white, cold and empty, …

In a forest:

At sea:

In a cave:

In space:

2.2 Where are they?

Read these two texts. Where is each person?

a.
It's dark, hot and damp here.
There are sounds all around me.
I feel so small. High above me I can
hear noises, animals calling.
The sun is shining through the
trees, sparkling against the
darkness of the leaves.

b.
There's nothing, nothing out here.
An enormous empty space with no
air, no people, no life. Below me
I can see a large rock, floating
and turning in the infinite space.
I can shout 'hello' but no one
can hear me. I'm alone, far from
our planet.

Now choose one of the places in Exercise 1 and write a short paragraph about what you can see, what you can hear and how you feel.

3 A story in sound

3.1 What's happening?

🔲 Listen to the cassette. What's happening? Make some notes about what you can hear.

3.2 A story

Listen to the sounds again and look at your notes. Can you write a short story about the sounds?

Some years ago, there was …

6

Ways to speaking and listening (1)

In this Unit you can see some
techniques to help you with speaking
and listening in English or in your
language.

1 Before you speak

When you want to say something, it is often
useful to prepare first! Here are some things
that you can do.

1.1 Plan what you want to say

Think about the words that you will need.
Use a dictionary and your books to help you.
What would you say in these situations?

a You want to ask someone in the street for
directions to the bus station, how far it is and
how long it takes to get there.

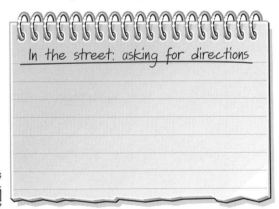

In the street: asking for directions

b You want to ask in a shop if they have a music
cassette that you want and how much it is. If
they don't have it, you want to order it.

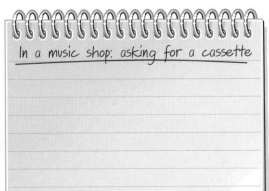

In a music shop: asking for a cassette

1.2 Predict what the other person might say

Now think about the language the other
person might use. Think about the situations
in Exercise 1.1. Predict!

a Someone in the street gives you directions

In the street: what they might say

b In a music shop

In a music shop: what they might say

Next lesson, compare your answers to
Exercises 1.1 and 1.2 with other students.

1.3 Talk to yourself!

Practise what you will say. Take both parts in the conversation.
Look at the situations in Exercise 1.1 again and talk to yourself!

Excuse me, can you tell me the way to the bus station?

Yes, of course. You go straight down the road and turn …

2 If you don't know the correct word …

If you don't know the correct word for something, you can explain instead. Can you match the phrases with the correct picture? Five phrases are missing. What can you say?

1 something to correct what you write

2 ....

3 something to help you draw a line

4 ....

5 something to draw a circle

6 ....

7 something to do your hair

8 ....

9 a small light for your hand

10 ....

7 Revision

Here are some things you learned to do in Units 3–6. How well can you do them? Put a tick (✓) in the box.

	I can do it:	very well	OK	a little
1 New words				
2 Past continuous				
3 Cause and effect, zero conditional				
4 Modals ('should,' 'mustn't,' 'might,' 'need to')				

Now choose some of these sections to revise and practise.

1 What's the word?

1.1 A puzzle

Write the correct word in the puzzle.

```
1 _ _ _        _ _ _ _ _ _
  2 _ _        _ _ _
3 _ _ _        _ _ _ _
    4          _ _ _ _ _ _ _ _
5 _ _          _ _
  6 _          _ _ _
7 _ _ _        _ _ _
  8 _          _ _ _
```

1 John Franklin was the leader of an Arctic e............ .

2 Franklin took a lot of l............ juice with him.

3 An i............ is a large piece of frozen water.

4 Magellan was an e............ .

5 Franklin was looking for a northwest r............ to Canada.

6 Australia exports a lot of s............ .

7 It is important to eat a lot of fresh f............ .

8 The liquid that comes from fruit is called j............ .

1.2 What does it mean?

Here are some adjectives from Units 3–6. Each adjective has lots of meanings 'in it'. Look at the table and put a tick (✓) if you think it has that meaning.

	means 'not normal'	means 'very good'	means 'not happy'	can describe people	can describe objects
strange	✓			✓	✓
excellent					
worried					
disturbed					
extreme					
perfect					
magic					

2 The *Hindenburg* in the news

Can you complete the newspaper article with the correct form of the verbs?

1 fly **2** happen **3** look **4** wait **5** film **6** crash **7** die
8 happen **9** fly **10** come **11** explode **12** start

Listen and check your answers.

Disaster in the air – the *Hindenburg* explodes

There was panic in New York last night as disaster hit the Hindenburg, the transatlantic airship. It **1** *was flying* from Germany to the United States when a terrible accident **2** .... In the airship, people **3** .... out of the window. On the ground, people **4** .... for the airship to arrive. Cameras **5** .... the airship for the news. Suddenly, there was an enormous explosion and the airship **6** .... to the ground in flames. Thirty-six people **7** .... in the accident. Nobody is sure why the accident **8** .... Some people say that there was a bomb on the airship. Experts, however, say that they think that there was a hydrogen leak. They think that while it **9** .... from Germany, static electricity probably formed around the airship. Then, when it **10** .... near the airship station, a spark jumped to the ground and the hydrogen **11** .... and **12** .... a fire.

3 Look after your bike!

Can you complete each sentence with a suitable modal?

must   needn't   need to   don't have to   should
shouldn't   mustn't

BICYCLES ARE GREAT! If you have a bicycle, you _____ walk everywhere. You can get to places much quicker and get exercise at the same time! Also, bicycles are cheap to run! You _____ spend money on petrol or parking. Here are some important points to remember.

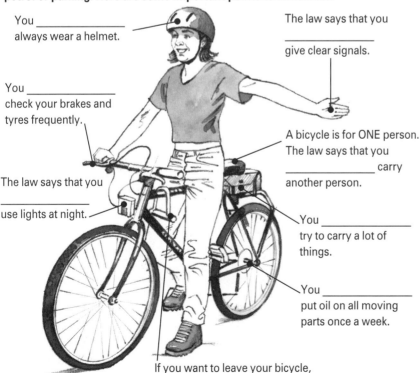

You _____ always wear a helmet.

You _____ check your brakes and tyres frequently.

The law says that you _____ use lights at night.

The law says that you _____ give clear signals.

A bicycle is for ONE person. The law says that you _____ carry another person.

You _____ try to carry a lot of things.

You _____ put oil on all moving parts once a week.

If you want to leave your bicycle, you _____ buy a lock.

4 Look after your health!

Look at the health leaflet. Can you complete each sentence?

Look after your health!

If you don't sleep enough,
....

If you don't have enough exercise,
....

If you smoke cigarettes,
....

If you eat too many fatty foods,
....

If you stay in the sun too much,
....

If you drink a lot of fizzy drinks,
....

If you don't wear warm clothes on a cold day,
....

A vocabulary map (1)
Exploration

Write these words in the correct area of the vocabulary map. (Some words can go in two or more areas.) You can also add the meanings in your language (in the bottom half of each box). Can you add any more words that you know or any more areas to the map?

collect dangerous death disappear discover disease
enormous equipment excellent expedition explore
explorer extreme cold extreme heat food hard hunt
illness jungle map mountain mystery perfect poisoning
rope route sail scientific instruments search ship sign
sink steal strange suffer survive tent terrible
the Antarctic the Arctic worried

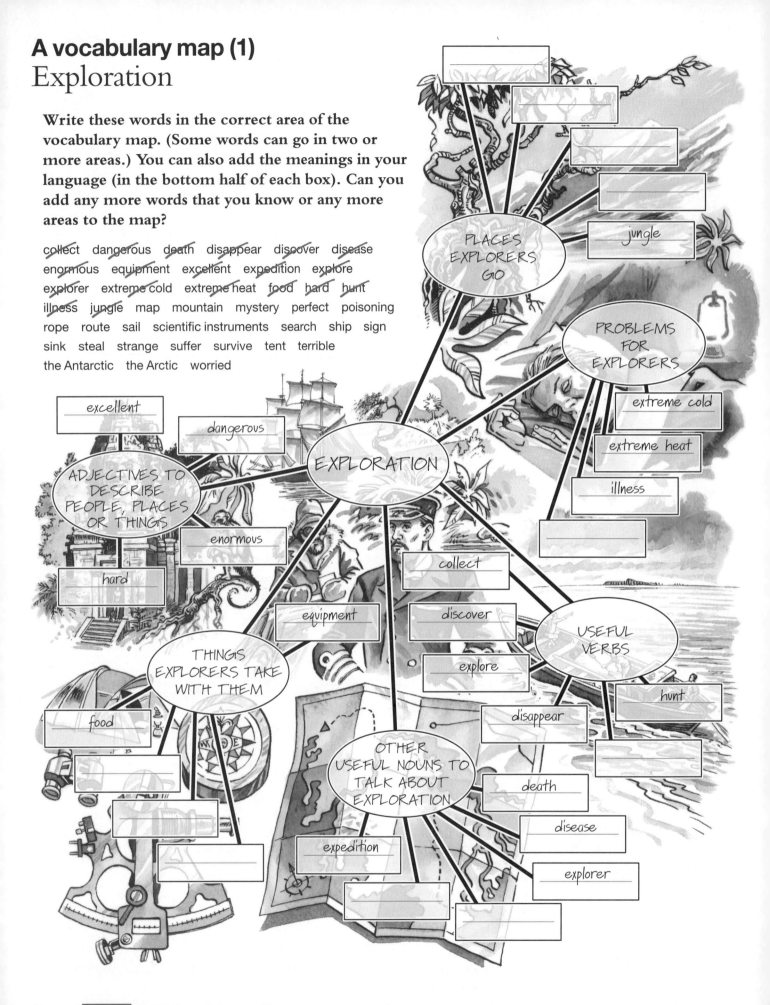

PLACES EXPLORERS GO

jungle

PROBLEMS FOR EXPLORERS

extreme cold

extreme heat

illness

ADJECTIVES TO DESCRIBE PEOPLE, PLACES OR THINGS

excellent

dangerous

enormous

hard

EXPLORATION

collect

discover

explore

USEFUL VERBS

hunt

disappear

equipment

THINGS EXPLORERS TAKE WITH THEM

food

OTHER USEFUL NOUNS TO TALK ABOUT EXPLORATION

death

disease

explorer

expedition

FOCUS ON

Our environment 8
Topic and language

THEME B

Vocabulary; pronunciation of '-tion' /ʃn/; Present perfect; reading

1 *Vocabulary*

2 /ʃn/

1 What's the word?

Read the clues 1–11 and write the correct word in the puzzle. What are the missing letters? What does the puzzle spell?

ultraviolet generator natural factory climate reduce health sprays future tree oil

1 A machine that makes electricity.
2 We have to find ways to .... pollution.
3 Oil, coal, wood, air and water are all .... resources.
4 Many people in cities now have .... problems.
5 .... is a thick, black liquid that comes from the ground.
6 The special type of oxygen around the Earth is important because it stops .... radiation.
7 Many aerosol .... destroy the atmosphere.
8 A place where they manufacture things.
9 We must change the way we live. We have to think about the ....
10 Many scientists say that the .... is changing.
11 A very large plant that helps to make oxygen.

2 Say it clearly

2.1 How to say '-tion'

Notice how you usually pronounce '-tion' in English.

pollution /pəˈluːʃn/ radiation /reɪdiˈeɪʃn/
information /ɪnfəˈmeɪʃn/

Read these words. Which one *doesn't* have the /ʃn/ sound?

pollution radiation information invention
exploration question condition expedition

Listen and check your answer. Say the words.

2.2 Say some sentences

Say some sentences with the /ʃn/ sound.

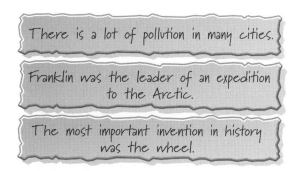

There is a lot of pollution in many cities.

Franklin was the leader of an expedition to the Arctic.

The most important invention in history was the wheel.

Say some more sentences of your own with words from Exercise 2.1

3 What a classroom!

Look at the picture. Is your classroom like this? What have the students just done? Write a sentence about each person in the picture.

(Notice how you can say 'just' to mean 'a few moments ago'.)

1 Helen has just broken her pencil.

2 Dave ....

3 Susan ....

4 Nahed ....

5 Kim ....

6 Val ....

7 Ingrid ....

8 Arifa ....

9 Steve ....

10 The teacher ....

4 Talk to Lewis

Write your answers to Lewis' questions. Then talk to him on the cassette.

LEWIS: Hello there! What have you done today?

YOU: ....

LEWIS: I've done a lot today. I've written two letters and I've finished a book. What have you read this week?

YOU: ....

LEWIS: I like reading. I also like watching films. Have you seen any films recently?

YOU: ....

LEWIS: What was the name of the last film you saw?

YOU: ....

LEWIS: Mmmm. I don't think I've seen that film. Was it good?

YOU: ....

LEWIS: Last week I was on holiday. I went to the mountains. Have you ever been to the mountains?

YOU: ....

LEWIS: What places have you visited in your country?

YOU: ....

LEWIS: Oh, really. When did you go there?

YOU: ....

LEWIS: That's interesting. For my next holiday, I'll try to visit those places. I have to go now. Bye.

YOU: ....

5 Look, no wheels!

Read more about the Maglev train.

THE FLYING TRAIN

One of the most exciting new types of train is the Maglev train. The Maglev train is very different from normal trains. It does not have any wheels. It uses magnetic levitation to float on the rail. It can travel very fast – over 500 kilometres an hour. It is very quiet and it is very clean. It doesn't have any wheels or any parts that move.

How does it work?

The secret is that it uses magnets in a new type of motor. Have you ever tried to push two magnets together? If you hold them one way, they attract each other. If you hold them the other way, they repel each other.

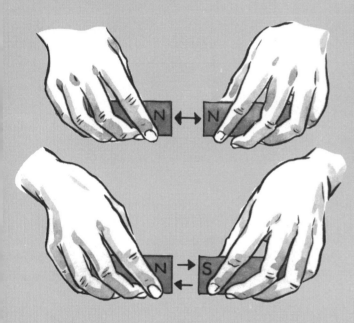

The Maglev train uses magnets in the same way. The motor is a very big electromagnet. (An electromagnet is a magnet that only works when there is electricity.) The electricity changes direction all the time and the magnet changes from north to south, south to north. There are more electromagnets on the rail and this pushes the train forward.

Why don't we see the Maglev train now?

The train is fast, quiet and clean. Why don't we see it everywhere now? Part of the answer is that the train can only take people. It cannot carry very heavy things. Also, because it goes so fast, the rail must be very straight. This makes it difficult to use it in places where there are a lot of hills. But the real answer is because it is very expensive to build. A long rail of electromagnets costs a lot of money. It also uses a lot of electricity. We need to find a cheaper, cleaner way to make electricity if we want to see 'The Flying Train' in our towns and cities.

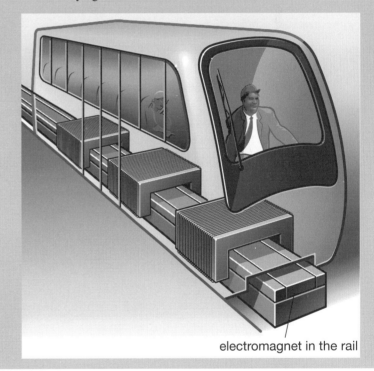

electromagnet in the rail

Is the information in these sentences true [T], false [F] or not in the text [?].

a The Maglev train cannot take heavy things. ☐

b The Maglev train can only go on straight rails. ☐

c The train makes a lot of noise. ☐

d There is a Maglev train in Japan. ☐

e The biggest problem for the Maglev train is that it is too expensive. ☐

f It is possible to use the Maglev train everywhere. ☐

g The train cannot work when it is raining. ☐

Listen to the text on the cassette.
Three pieces of information are missing.
What are they?

a ....

b ....

c ....

Vocabulary;
Future simple;
first conditional

1 *Vocabulary*

2 *Reading and writing; Future simple and first conditional*

3 *Future simple*

4 *Writing and speaking*

9 Save the Earth!
Topic and language

1 What's the word?

Read the clues. Can you find the words in the dustbin?

1 Things that we do not want anymore:
   r..............................

2 If we turn off lights when we are not using them, we can s.............................. energy.

3 We have to find ways to r.............................. the things that we use. For example, we can use paper again.

4 Plastic is not b.............................. This means it will not disappear for hundreds of years.

5 Many of the things that we buy come with too much p...............................

6 Motor cars p.............................. the atmosphere.

7 Coal, gas, oil and minerals are natural r...............................

8 We have to find a.............................. ways to make electricity.

9 A lot of the things that we produce are u...............................

10 People in the USA use almost 70 times more e.............................. every day than people in India.

Find some more words in Unit 9 and make a word square for other students. Write some clues in English and some clues in your language.

```
B A W R T Y P O L L U T E
I L C V Y J K I O P N E G
O T V P A C K A G I N G K
D E H Y U I S A V E E M N
E R R W R X V B J K C I F
G N U R E S O U R C E S D
R A B Q C W C B N M S R E
A T B X Y X L I T A S T J
D I I A C X C G H Y A V N
A V S W L T N J O B R R B
B E H Q E N E R G Y Y E W
L E T W U K P Q D N M W Z
E U O Q S R V J K L P U I
```

2 If ...

2.1 Changes in the future

In your Student's Book you saw what will happen to our cities if the temperature rises. If the temperature rises, the climate will also change. Can you put these sentences in the correct order?

☐ a If agriculture changes, we will have to eat different things.

☐ b If we have to eat different things, our lives will change a lot.

[2] c If the temperature rises, the climate will change.

☐ d If plants and crops don't grow in the same way, agriculture will change.

[1] e If carbon dioxide in the air increases, the temperature will rise a lot.

☐ f If the winds and rain change, plants and crops will not grow in the same way.

☐ g If the climate changes, the winds and rain will change.

2.2 Think!

Choose some of these questions and write about what you think will happen. Write three or four sentences for each one. Look at Exercise 2.1 for ideas.

> What will happen if we don't have enough water in the future?

> What will happen if the air is not good outside?

> *What will happen if there are too many cars?*

> **What will happen if we don't have any coal, gas or oil?**

> *What will happen if everybody works at home?*

> What will happen if cities grow to 100 million people?

Compare your ideas with other students next lesson.

3 What do they think?

🎧 Some students asked people what they think about life in the year 2100. Listen. What does each person say? Copy and complete the table.

	Person 1	Person 2	Person 3
How will we live? Will life be better or worse?			

4 Talk to Maggi

🎧 Write your answers to Maggi's questions. Then talk to her on the cassette.

MAGGI: Hi. Do you live in a big town?

YOU: ....

MAGGI: Well, I live in a big town in California. There is quite a lot of pollution here. Is there a lot of pollution where you live?

YOU: ....

MAGGI: One good thing in my town is that we have some big parks. What about where you live?

YOU: ....

MAGGI: That's interesting. At my school, we are collecting old aluminium cans to recycle them. Are you doing anything in your school like that?

YOU: ....

MAGGI: In my town, there are lots of 'bottle banks' where you can take old bottles. Do you have them near where you live?

YOU: ....

MAGGI: What other things do people do to help the environment where you live?

YOU: ....

MAGGI: In the US, there are special laws to control pollution. What special laws are there in your country?

YOU: ....

MAGGI: That's interesting. Can you tell me some more about that?

YOU: ....

MAGGI: Well, I must go now. Talk to you later! Bye.

10 Earth poems
Fluency

1 Miriam's poems

Miriam likes writing short poems about her ideas. She has written some poems about the Earth. Read each one. In which poem do you think she feels:

happy? angry? worried?

You can listen to the poems on the cassette.

The bus
This morning
I was walking to school.
I was thinking about things,
I was looking at the people on the street,
When, suddenly, I saw it.

A large old bus.
It was going slowly up the hill.
Inside, there were people.
They were talking.
They were laughing.
They didn't know what was happening.

Behind them there was a big black cloud.
Black and dirty, coming from the bus.
It filled the air,
My eyes, my lungs, my clothes.
I ran ahead but the bus went faster.

Then it stopped.
The people got off, laughing and talking.
They didn't know that I saw a crime.
And they were in it.

Some trees in California
There are some trees in California.
They are over 4,000 years old.
They are tall and strong.
Can you imagine what they have seen?
Four thousand years!
They have seen earthquakes.
They have seen the Native Americans, living all alone.
They have seen millions of people come and go.
They have seen animals disappear for ever.
And now they see us.
Will the trees live another 4,000 years?
Another 400 years?
Another 4 years?
We must decide now.

Life is full of surprises
It's so beautiful today.
The sun has risen.
The birds have woken up.
The day has begun.

I wonder …
What will I do today?
Where will I go?
Who will I meet?
What will I learn?

Life will be full of surprises
On a beautiful day like today!

2 What is she saying?

Read *The bus* and *Some trees in California* again carefully. Write your answers to these questions.

The bus

What is 'it' in line 5? ....

She says 'They didn't know what was happening'. What *was* happening? ....

Who is 'them' in line 12? ....

What is 'it' in line 17? ....

What was the 'crime'? ....

What is 'it' in line 20? ....

Some trees in California

What other things do you think the trees have seen? Write three or four more sentences.

3 Your own poem

GOLDEN RULES FOR WRITING POEMS
1 ANYONE can write poems.
2 Poems don't have to rhyme.
3 There aren't 'good poems' or 'bad poems'. Poems are YOUR ideas.
4 You don't have to write in complete sentences.
5 Experiment! Change things while you are writing.

You can write your own poem about life on Earth. Write about the ideas that *you* have in *your* head Think about:

the seasons   animals and plants you have seen
what people are doing to the Earth   the sun, the moon, the sky
what you will do tomorrow … anything!

You can follow these steps to help you.

a First make some notes.

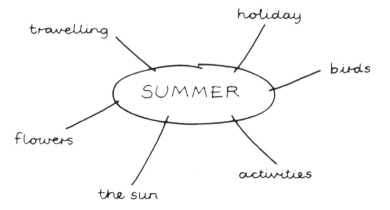

b Next write some ideas.

SUMMER

It's summer soon.
Holidays in the sun.
At home, with the family.
Travelling to new places.

c Read what you have written. Make changes as you write.

SUMMER

It's summer soon.
Long days
Holidays in the sun.
friends
At home, with the family.
Travelling to new places.

d Write your poem on a clean piece of paper. Add some drawings or pictures.

11 Ways to writing (1): getting ideas

In this Unit, you can see some techniques to help you with writing. You can use these techniques when you are writing in English or in your language. You can also use these techniques just to get ideas for things.

1 Ways of getting ideas

Sometimes it is difficult to start writing. Here are some techniques for getting ideas. Have you seen them before?

Brainstorms

Think about the topic and make notes. You can also ask questions: *Why? When? How? Where? What?*

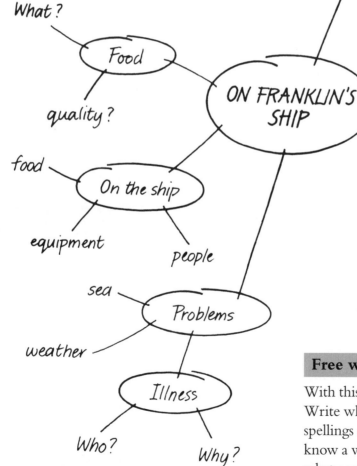

Free writing

With this technique you just write. Don't stop. Write what is in your head. Don't think about spellings or grammar. Just write. If you don't know a word, write it in your language. Write what comes into your head about the topic … keep the ideas coming!

Free notes

Think about the topic and write notes on a piece of paper. Write them anywhere on the paper. When you have finished, you can organise your notes.

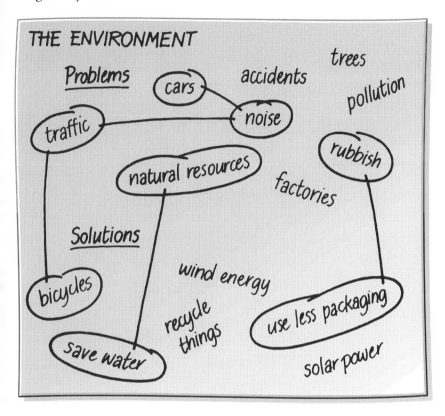

3 Write!

Choose one of your topics and write one or two paragraphs about it. Use your notes to help you. Keep your work for Workbook Unit 16.

2 Your ideas

Look at this list of topics. Choose three topics (or invent your own) and make notes about each one. Use a different technique for each topic.

Next lesson, compare notes with other students.

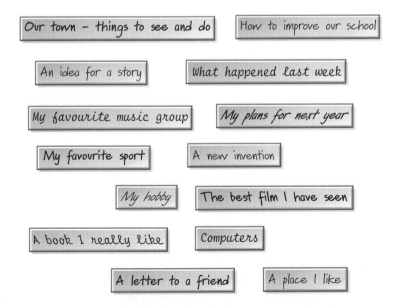

A test on Units
8–11

1 *Vocabulary*

2 *Present perfect*

3 *Future simple;
first
conditional*

4 *Offers with
'will'*

12 Test yourself

Here are some things you learned to do in Units 8–11.

How well can you do them? Put a tick (✓) in the box.

I can do it:	very well	OK	a little
1 Use the new words			
2 Talk about a past action with present result (Present perfect)			
3 Talk about the future ('will')			
4 Make offers			

Now do this test and see if you are right.

1 Into the ground!

Look at the puzzle. Can you find 10 words from Units 8–11? They begin with these letters:

d .... p .... p ....
p .... p .... r ....
r .... b .... c ....
c ....

Now complete the text with words from the puzzle.

LANDFILLS

People in the USA (1) ....*produce*........ about 2 kg each of (2) .... every day. Most of this goes into big holes in the ground called 'landfills'.

Landfills don't solve the problem of rubbish – they hide it. Things like paper and food, for example, are (3) .... but the process is very slow. Things like metal and (4) .... never disappear. Landfills also cause water (5) .... because dangerous (6) .... often come out into the rivers.

We have to stop producing so much rubbish! At the moment, everything we buy has too much (7) .... We (8) .... only about 13% of our paper and cans but we could increase this to 45%.

There are two extra words in the puzzle. Use the words to write two sentences about alternatives for the future.

....
....

```
B D E S T R O Y V F D C
I P C H E M I C A L S Y
O O R C O N S U M E F S
D L E F U I O P N S P J
E L C F T Y U K L M A F
G U Y P R O D U C E F D
R T C B R U S B K J L A
A I L H O J S E G A R V
D O E X Y U I O P P L A
A N H P A C K A G I N G
B A L U E J N K T L V E
L R U B B I S H I O N F
E B H P L A S T I C H H
```

2 A landfill archaeologist

Charles Watson has an unusual job. He is a landfill archaeologist. Steven Black is talking to him about his work. Read Charles' answers and write Steven's questions.

STEVEN: How long [1] .... a landfill archaeologist?

CHARLES: About 20 years, I think.

STEVEN: What do you do, exactly?

CHARLES: I investigate landfills. I also see how landfills have changed. It's a very important job!

STEVEN: How [2] ....
..............................?

CHARLES: Well, they have changed in many ways. They are a lot bigger nowadays.

STEVEN: Why?

CHARLES: Well, in the past, people sold things or tried to repair them. Now they just throw them away. People also throw away a lot more food.

STEVEN: Have [3] .... any old food?

CHARLES: Oh yes, we often discover old food. Nearly every day we discover food that is 15 or 20 years old – meat, vegetables, bread. Food has a lot of chemicals in it now to preserve it, so it isn't so biodegradable.

STEVEN: [4] ....?

CHARLES: Oh! I've found lots of valuable things. Watches, rings, cameras – all sorts of things!

STEVEN: [5] ....?

CHARLES: Well, I haven't found much money!

STEVEN: Thanks, Charles.

CHARLES: Nice talking to you, Steven.

Listen and check your answers.

3 What will happen?

Finish the sentences with your own words.

1 If we recycle all our paper ....

2 If we reduce the amount of packaging
....

3 If we don't use plastic bags ....

4 If we manufacture electric cars we will
....

4 I'll help!

You want to help these people. What can you say?

a ....

b ....

c ....

d ....

A vocabulary map (2)

The environment

Write these words in the correct area of the vocabulary map. (Some words can go in two or more areas.) You can also add the meanings in your language (in the bottom half of each box). Can you add any more words that you know or any more areas to the map?

acid rain   avoid   building   burn   car   carbon dioxide   cattle
climate   cycle   farm   field   grass   house   pavement   plant
pollute   pollution   radiation   recycle   reduce   river   road
rubbish   sheep   smog   steam   street   take action
the greenhouse effect   the ozone layer   throw away   traffic
traffic light   traffic sign   tree   ultraviolet light

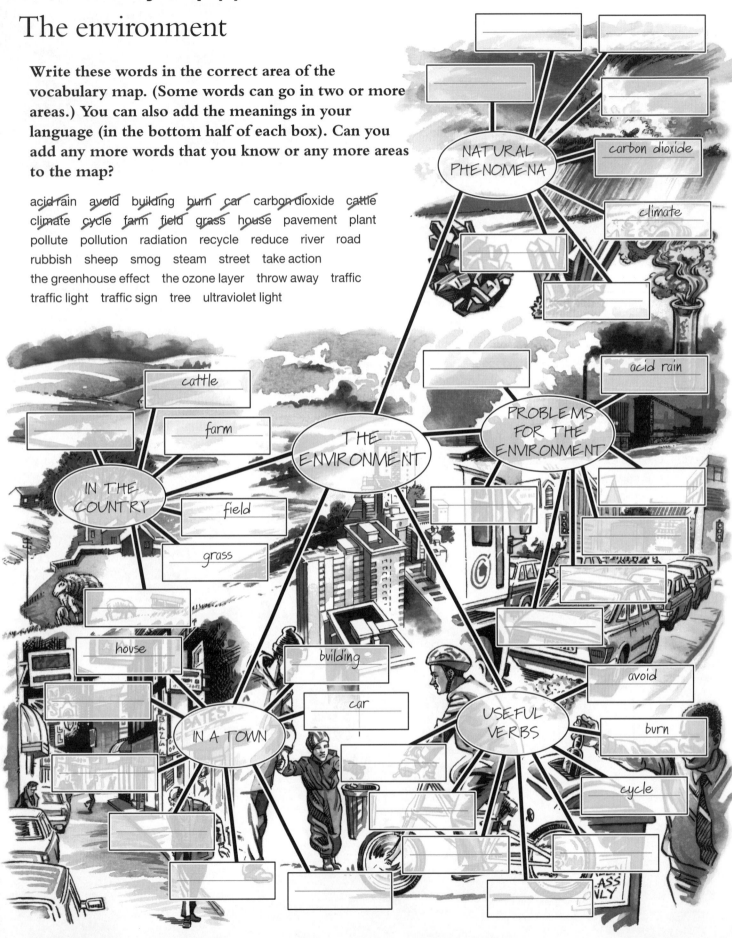

NATURAL PHENOMENA

carbon dioxide

climate

acid rain

PROBLEMS FOR THE ENVIRONMENT

cattle

farm

THE ENVIRONMENT

IN THE COUNTRY

field

grass

house

building

car

IN A TOWN

USEFUL VERBS

avoid

burn

cycle

FOCUS ON
Music 13
Topic and language

1 *Vocabulary: musical instruments*

1 Some musical instruments

We often think about musical instruments in different categories. Look at the pictures. Can you write the names of the instruments under the correct heading?

Violin

Instruments that have strings (Stringed instruments)	Instruments that we blow (Wind instruments)
Instruments that we hit (Percussion instruments)	Instruments, that have 'keys' (Keyboard instruments)

saxophone

organ

piano

marimba

double bass

tubular bells

Now look at the instruments in Exercise 1 in your Student's Book.
Put them under the correct heading.

flute

2 Some types of music

2.1 Descriptions and pictures

Read about some different types of music. Can you match them to the correct picture?

Raga a form of music from India. Ragas are often played on a sitar. They often express feelings about the seasons, times of the day, emotions and places.

Calypso a form of music and dance from Trinidad, West Indies. Calypso is often played at carnival time, when people dance in the streets. Steel bands often play calypso rhythms on drums made from oil containers.

Classical music Most people use the term 'classical music' to mean serious music, in contrast to popular music. In fact, 'classical' means a style in music history, from about 1750 to 1825. Beethoven, Mozart and Haydn were all great classical composers.

a

Blues a form of music invented by black Americans in the late 1800s. Blues musicians often sang about love, hard work and poverty and played the guitar or piano. Today, blues music is played by black and white musicians all over the world.

Samba a type of music and dance from Brazil, that originally came from Africa. Samba music has strong rhythms, in which people sing and play percussion instruments. It is a group dance, where people often dance in a circle.

b

c

d

e

2.2 Musical extracts

Can you match each piece of music on the cassette to the pictures and description in Exercise 2.1?

Listen and write the name of the type of music.

1 ....

2 ....

3 ....

4 ....

5 ....

3 A busy evening

Last night some friends came to Peter's house. Look carefully at the picture. Can you find eight things that he had done before they arrived? Write a sentence about each one (use the list of irregular verbs in your Student's Book). For example:

He had cut his hair.

4 Say it clearly

4.1 Listen and say the words

There are three ways to say '-ed' at the end of verbs or adjectives from verbs. Listen and say the words.

After verbs that end with /t/ or /d/, you say /ɪd/

hated started ended mended

After verbs that end with /p/, /k/, /tʃ/, /f/, /θ/, /s/ or /ʃ/, you say /t/

stopped liked washed introduced

After verbs that end with a vowel or /b/, /l/, /g/, /v/, /z/, /ɜː/, /m/, /n/, /ŋ/, /dʒ/, you say /d/

arrived lived listened played

4.2 /t/, /d/ or /ɪd/?

Can you put these verbs into the correct column?

asked changed climbed decided developed discovered
dropped happened looked stayed studied visited wanted
watched

liked /t/	lived /ɪd/	started /d/

Listen and check your answers with the cassette.

5 Talk to Lewis

Write your answers to Lewis' questions. Then talk to him on the cassette.

LEWIS: Hi! How are you today?

YOU: ....

LEWIS: Do you want to hear my new cassette? Listen. Do you like it?

YOU: ....

LEWIS: Well, I think it's awful! It was a free gift with a magazine. What type of music do you like?

YOU: ....

....

LEWIS: Can you give me some examples?

YOU: ....

....

LEWIS: That's interesting. I like playing the guitar. Do you play a musical instrument?

YOU: ....

LEWIS: What is your favourite instrument?

YOU: ....

LEWIS: Why?

YOU: ....

....

LEWIS: Sometimes, I listen to music when I'm doing my homework. When do you listen to music?

YOU: ....

LEWIS: Well, I must go now. It was nice to talk to you. Bye!

14 The big screen
Topic and language

1 What's it about?

1.1 Types of films

Can you match each type of film to the topics on the screen?

a western film
a detective film
a horror film
a romance film
an action film
a historical film
a science fiction film

is usually about

creatures from other planets
the supernatural
solving a crime
love
cowboys in the USA
EVENTS LONG AGO
DANGEROUS EVENTS

1.2 A film guide

Read about three films. What type of film is each one?

Journey: ....
22nd Street: ....
In the night: ....

Film Guide

JOURNEY is about two men and two women who are travelling to another planet. The journey goes well until there is a serious problem with the computer. At first they think that the computer has gone wrong but they soon discover that it is functioning perfectly well. The problem is that they don't have control over it.
★★★★

22ND STREET Another film about Inspector Kogan. Builders are knocking down a house in 22nd Street when they discover a large heavy box. Inside, there are paintings thousands of years old. Kogan goes to 22nd Street and starts an investigation and discovers a trail of murder and robbery that goes back 200 years.
★★★

IN THE NIGHT Late one night, Steven Jackson is driving home from work when he sees a strange light in front of him. He stops the car and as he gets out he hears terrible screams. Two bright red eyes are looking at him through the darkness and Jackson's problems begin. A slow-moving film.
★★

2 Making Superman fly

Read about how they make Superman fly in the film. Can you complete the text with a gerund after each preposition?

Making Superman fly

Special effects people are very good at _making_ (make) things look real. By
[1] .... (use) special techniques, they can make monsters move and talk, buildings burn and even entire planets explode.

In films like Superman, for example, special effects people are responsible for [2] .... (make) Superman 'fly'. Instead of
[3] .... (hang) him from an aeroplane, they build a special system with a screen and mirrors.

First, artists are responsible for [4] .... (paint) the background. Then, they film the painting. By [5] .... (zoom) in and out they can make it bigger or smaller.

Next, the set builders have the job of
[6] .... (build) a screen with a large metal 'arm' in the middle. When they have done that, they put Superman on the metal arm.

The camera people are now in charge of
[7] .... (film) Superman. By
[8] .... (use) mirrors, they project the background picture on to the screen. A camera then films Superman as he is 'flying' over the city.

By [9] .... (zoom) out and in, they can make Superman fly higher or lower over the city. Only the camera lens moves – Superman doesn't move at all!

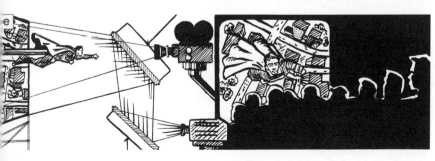

3 Say it clearly

3.1 Weak prepositions

In English, prepositions are normally 'weak', without stress. For example, instead of saying 'for' as /fɔː/ we say /f ə/. Listen and say these sentences.

> I haven't seen her for a week. She went on holiday for a few days.

3.2 Some more examples

Read these sentences and underline the prepositions. (There are nine prepositions.)

> Are you interested in seeing a film?
> There's a good film on at the cinema.
> It's about life in the future.
> The people live under the ground.
> Instead of eating food, they eat tablets with lots of protein.

Listen carefully to the sentences. Then, play them again and say them.

4 Making a storm in the sea

Sometimes they want to show a large ship in the sea, perhaps in a violent storm. How do they do that? Look at the pictures and explain what they do.

a First, they ....

b Then, ...

c Next, ...

d When they have done that, they ....

e Finally, they ....

f If they want a storm, they ....

a model of the ship

a

a tank of water

b

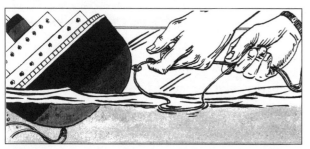

c

a high speed camera

d

A normal speed projector. This makes the ship look big and heavy.

e

fans

detergent

f

5 Talk to Maggi

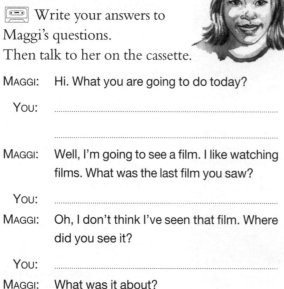

Write your answers to Maggi's questions.
Then talk to her on the cassette.

MAGGI: Hi. What you are going to do today?

YOU: ....

....

MAGGI: Well, I'm going to see a film. I like watching films. What was the last film you saw?

YOU: ....

MAGGI: Oh, I don't think I've seen that film. Where did you see it?

YOU: ....

MAGGI: What was it about?

YOU: ....

....

....

MAGGI: That's interesting. What happened in the film?

YOU: ....

....

....

MAGGI: Did you like it?

YOU: ....

MAGGI: Mmm. Perhaps I'll see it one day. What type of films do you like most?

YOU: ....

MAGGI: I like science fiction films. That's what I'm going to see today. I must go now. See you later!

On an island 15

Fluency

1 **What should you do?**

Imagine …
You were on a small boat with some friends when suddenly it hit some rocks. The boat sank immediately but you all swam to an island. You're now on the island. You can't stay on the beach because it's too hot. What should you do? Read card 1, decide what you are going to do and choose the next card.

① In front of you there is a thick jungle. You don't know if there are any people on the island but you know that people live on the next island which isn't far away. What should you do next?

Card 8: Should you go into the jungle and see if there are any people there?
Card 5: Should you build a simple raft and try to cross to the next island?

② The raft stayed together but the weather suddenly became bad. The wind was very strong and the waves have taken you back to the beach. The weather is better now so you can start again with a new raft or go into the jungle. *Go to card 1.*

③ It was very difficult in the jungle but you are now much nearer the building. Unfortunately, in front of you there is an enormous ravine and you can't get across. What should you do?

Card 6: You could build a bridge.
Card 7: You could try to swing across with ropes made from plants.

④ The raft is a disaster. It has fallen apart completely. The only thing you can do is to go back to the beach as quickly as you can and start again. *Go to card 1.*

(5) You have built a simple raft but there are a lot of sharks in the water. The next island is not far away but you are not sure if you can get there easily. What should you do?

Card 9: Should you try to cross on the raft?

Card 10: Should you try a route into the jungle first?

(6) Disaster! You built a bridge and tried to cross on it but it collapsed. You fell down a long way and you can't get back up. One of your friends has a broken leg and can't move. But you can hear a car or lorry – there are people on the island! All you can do is shout loudly and hope that they can hear you …

(9) You got on the raft and everything went fine at first but now it is very rough and there are sharks all around you. You think the raft is too big and it could sink. What should you do?

Card 4: You can divide the raft into smaller sections and try to continue individually.

Card 2: You can all stay on one raft and hope for the best.

(7) You crossed over the ravine without any problem. It is now much easier to walk through the jungle and you have discovered a road. In front of you, you can see some houses and there is smoke coming from a chimney. You're nearly home!

(10) You have found an easy route through the jungle but you have come to an enormous river. It is a long way down to the river and the water is running very fast and there are many rocks. You think it's too dangerous to swim. What should you do?

Card 4: You can try to use a raft to get across.

Card 6: You can build a bridge.

(8) It is very difficult to move in the jungle. The plants are very thick and there are many dangerous animals. There is an old building in the distance. It looks empty. You are very tired and very weak and you have only a small bottle of water. What should you do next?

Card 3: Should you continue through the jungle?

Card 10: Should you try to find a better route?

2 Your own story

You can write your own adventure story. Work with some other students and plan your story. You can each write a different part.

(Hint: look carefully at the story in Exercise 1 to see how it works.)

Ways to writing (2): checking your work

16

In this Unit, you can see some more techniques to help you with writing. **IMPORTANT! You will need your work from Unit 11 (see Unit 11, Exercise 3).**

1 Check what you write!

When you write something, it is important to check your work. You can do this in different ways. Try this now with your work from Unit 11.

You can ask a friend

Read your work and make a list of things you want to check. Then ask a friend. For example:

'Is the grammar in this sentence correct?'
'Is this the correct spelling?'
'Is this clear to you?'
'How can I make it better?'
'Can I add something?'

You can check the language

Check different things in your work. Here are some lists.

ORGANISATION
Are the ideas in a logical order?
Are the paragraphs too long or short?
Should you use alternative words?

GRAMMAR
Are the verbs in the right form?
Are the words in the right order?
Are the prepositions correct?
Are the articles correct ('a' and 'the')?

SPELLING
For example:
plurals (e.g. '-y' to '-ies')
silent letters (e.g. ca*l*m)
double consonants (sto*pp*ing)
'h' in 'with' (NOT ~~wiht~~), 'the' (NOT ~~teh~~)

PUNCTUATION
capital letters at the beginning of sentences and names of people and places
full stops at the end of sentences
commas
apostrophes ('isn't', 'can't')

You can read it in different ways

Sometimes you can notice things if you read your work in different ways. For example:

Read it upside down

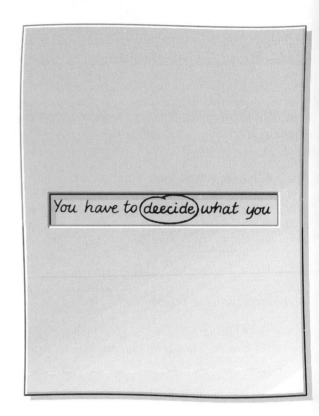

Read it through a 'window'

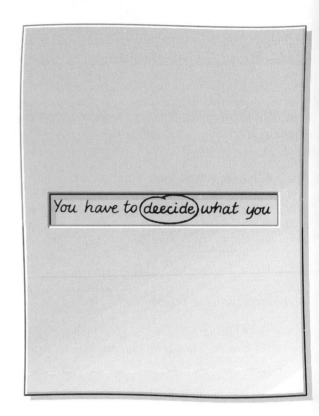

2 Learn from your mistakes!

Often, people make the same mistakes again and again when they write. Look back at all your writing in English. Make a list of your frequent mistakes. Use your list to correct your work next time. It helps!

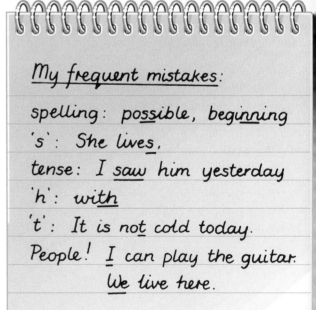

Revision

17

Here are some things you learned to do in Units 13–16. How well can you do them? Put a tick (✓) in the box.

Now choose some sections to revise and practise.

I can do it:	very well	OK	a little
1 Use the new vocabulary			
2 Past perfect (I *had done* that before)			
3 Explaining a process (First, …, Next, …)			
4 Gerunds (I am good *at* swimm*ing*)			

1 The words you met

Can you find the word on the CD? (The end of each word is the beginning of the next word.)

1 'Gospel' is a type of black r............ music.

2 'R & B' music had strong r............ that you could dance to.

3 A lot of rock music is very l............

4 A type of instrument from India.

5 A type of musical instrument that you blow.

6 A rock group's instruments are usually two or three guitars and a set of ....

7 It can t............ many months to record new songs.

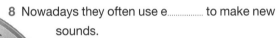

8 Nowadays they often use e............ to make new sounds.

9 Rock groups r............ their songs in a studio.

10 The Beatles had an important influence on the s............ of popular music.

11 The Beatles were very p............ They sold millions of records.

12 The opposite of 'loud'.

13 The person who cuts and checks the recording in a studio.

14 To grow or change.

2 I had never done that before!

Tony has just come back from an unusual trip. What is he telling his friend? Write a sentence for each picture.

It was fantastic! I did so many things, I had never drunk from an oasis before. I had never …

a **a** I had never drunk from an oasis before.

b ....

c ....

d ....

e ....

f ....

a

b

c

d

e

f

3 How do they make a tyrannosaurus move?

Look at the pictures and explain how they make a tyrannosaurus move in the cinema.

First, …

....

....

Then, …

....

....

Next, …

....

....

Then, …

....

....

They do this many times. When they have finished, they …

....

....

Finally, …

....

....

The tyrannosaurus moves!

🔲 Listen and check your answers.

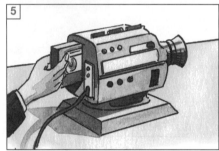

4 The stunt actors

Read about stunt actors. Put a circle around the preposition and then complete the text with a gerund.

🔲 Listen and check your answers.

Dangerous work for stunt actors

Most 'film stars' do not want to do dangerous things. They are afraid (of) ....*hurting*........ (hurt) themselves! Instead, the director employs 'stunt' actors who are expert at [1] .... (do) difficult and dangerous acts. For example, if the 'star' has to fall from a horse, a stunt actor who specialises in [2] .... (work) with horses does it instead. The stunt actor has the job of [3] .... (fall) from the horse without [4] .... (injure) himself. By [5] .... (film) the face of the 'star' and the body of the stunt actor, the director tricks us into [6] .... (think) that the 'star' is really doing it.

A vocabulary map (3)
The world of music and film

Write these words in the correct area of the vocabulary map. (Some words can go in two or more areas.) You can also add the meanings in your language (in the bottom half of each box). Can you add any more words that you know or any more areas to the map?

~~action~~ ~~actor, actress~~ ~~attract~~ ~~cartoon~~ ~~classical~~ ~~combine~~ ~~create~~
~~detective~~ develop ~~director~~ disco drums editor flute guitar
horror influence jazz mix organise popular producer record
recorder reggae rock rock'n'roll special effects people
synthesiser trumpet violin western writer

PEOPLE WHO MAKE FILMS

actor, actress

TYPES OF MUSIC

classical

THE WORLD OF MUSIC AND FILM

TYPES OF FILMS

action

cartoon

detective

TYPES OF MUSICAL INSTRUMENTS

USEFUL VERBS

attract

combine

create

18 FOCUS ON Change
Topic and language

1 What's the word?

Read the clues and write the correct word in the puzzle. What does the puzzle spell?

agriculture	average	cruel	election	earn	female
logical	rural	salary	urban	vote	wealthy

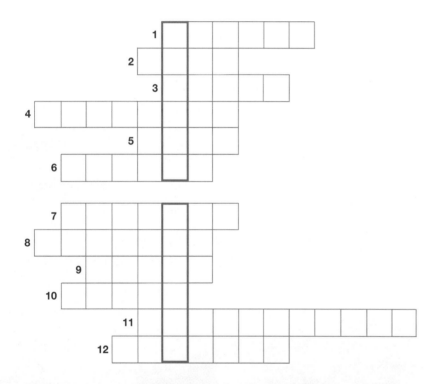

1 The money people receive every month when they are working.
2 In an election, people ....
3 In traditional stories, there is often one person who is very ....
4 In many countries, there is an .... every four years so that the people can choose the government.
5 Many people .... very little money every month.
6 The opposite of 'male' is '.....................................' .
7 Somebody who thinks carefully, step by step, is very ....
8 The gap between .... people and poor people is getting bigger everywhere.
9 In many countries, people move away from the .... areas to look for work in the towns.
10 Many .... areas are now very overpopulated.
11 In developed countries, more people work in industry than in ....
12 On .... women live five years longer than men.

2 Don't say it clearly!

2.1 Consonants and vowels

🔲 In English, people often join consonants and vowels together when they speak. (Vowel sounds are usually written with *a, e, i, o* and *u*. Consonants are all the other sounds.)

Listen and say these examples.

Look͜ at͜ South͜ America͜ lots͜ of things to͜ do

Look͜ at this postcard͜ of Rio.

Rio's͜ an͜ enormous city in South͜ America. The

beaches͜ are very beautiful and there͜ are lots͜ of

things to do there.

2.2 Join the vowel and the consonant

Join the vowel and the consonant in these phrases.

a block of flats   a week or two

a map of the world   a hard exam

a bar of chocolate   a can of juice

Make a sentence with each phrase and say them aloud.

3   Girls and boys at school

3.1 School subjects

This newspaper article is about examination results. Before you read, make a list of the subjects you do at school. Who does best at each subject – boys or girls?

🖭 Now read (and listen to) the article. Compare it with your ideas.

WHO DOES BETTER AT SCHOOL –
girls or boys?

This year's examination results show that girls are doing better than boys at the age of 16. Twenty years ago, girls used to get better results in languages and History and the boys used to get higher marks in Maths and the Sciences. Now, girls are doing better in all subjects. There are many possible reasons why this has happened.

Girls have to be twice as good
Amanda, 17, from Bristol says:
'Girls don't just want to get married now. They want to be independent. If you want a good job you have to work hard at school.'

Amanda's friend, Cathy, says:
'It's more difficult for women to get good jobs. They have to be twice as good as men to get the same job. We have to work harder!'

Work during the year
Mrs Armitage, a Chemistry teacher, comments:
'Ten years ago students used to get marks only for the examination but now they get marks for their work during the year. I think girls are more constant in their study so they often get higher average marks.'

Mr Evans, a Maths teacher, adds:
'In my experience, girls are serious about doing their homework. Boys are usually more interested in computer games and football!'

The exams
Ms Stephens, a head teacher, says:
'The exams have changed too. We used to ask students to remember a lot of facts but now they have to think more and give their own ideas. In general, girls seem to be better at this than boys.'

3.2 What do you think?

Some things in the article are FACTS. Other things are OPINIONS. Read the article again and <u>underline</u> the <u>opinions</u>. (Be careful! Opinions often look like facts!) Do you agree with each opinion? Write what you think. For example:

'Boys are usually more interested in computer games and football!'
I don't think this is true! A lot of boys ...

4 'used to'

5 Writing and speaking

4 Life then and now

Look at this information about differences between life in 1750 and today.

Look at the chart and write about the changes. You can use these phrases:

get married   have children   earn £X per month
work X hours per week

Life for factory workers in the UK:	1750	today
marry at:	26	24
die at:	48	77
most frequent reason for death:	smallpox	cancer
children:	10	2.1
wages per month:	£1.40	£640
working hours per week:	82	39

Life for factory workers today in the UK is very different from 1750. Today, factory workers earn about £640 per month but in 1750 they used to earn ...

5 Talk to Maggi

Write your answers to Maggi's questions. Then talk to her on the cassette.

MAGGI: Hi! What have you done today?

YOU: ....

MAGGI: Well, I looked at some old photos. My parents said when I was a baby I never used to sleep. What were you like as a baby?

YOU: ....

MAGGI: Oh, yes? I've got lots of photos of me at school. I remember I used to cry because I didn't understand Math. Did you use to be good at Math?

YOU: ....

MAGGI: My favourite subjects were Art and Science. What did you use to like at school?

YOU: ....

MAGGI: We used to live in the east of the United States then. Did you use to live in another town?

YOU: ....

MAGGI: Oh, that's interesting. I've got to go now. Talk to you soon. Bye!

Seeing is believing
Topic and language

19

Perception and
the brain;
relative clauses;
reading;
connected
speech

1 *Vocabulary*

1 What's the word?

Look at the clues and write the correct word in the puzzle. What does it spell?

believe	bends	blind	brain	clearly
diagonal	dot	guess	message	mirage
object	pattern	recognise	saucer	trick

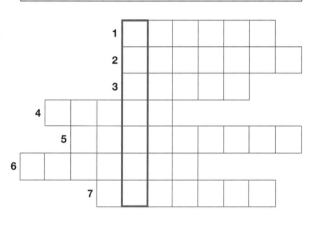

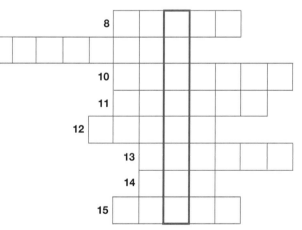

1 Have you ever seen a 'UFO' – an unidentified flying .... ?

2 This is a ....

3 Light can play a .... on our eyes.

4 This is a ....

5 I've changed the colour of my hair. You won't .... me!

6 When we see something our eyes send a .... to the brain.

7 When we can't see something .... our brain helps us to guess what it is.

8 People who cannot see are ....

9 This is a .... line.

10 We can't always .... what we see.

11 Look! A flying .... !

12 'How old are you?' '.....................................!'

13 In the desert, people often see a .... They think it's water but it's just the heat and the light.

14 This is a ....

15 Look! Light .... when it passes from air to water.

2 What can you see?

2.1 The way you look at it

Look at the pictures. You can see two or three different things in each one if you look carefully. What are they? Write a title for each one.

1

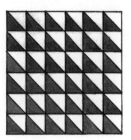

....

....

2

....

....

3

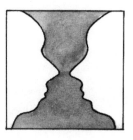

....

....

4

....

....

2.2 Optical illusions

What does your brain think when you look at these drawings? How are they really? Write a sentence about each one.

A

B

Line B looks as if it is longer than line A, but in reality they are the same length.

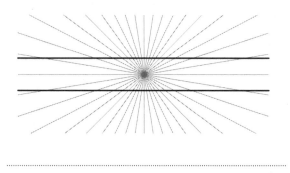

....

....

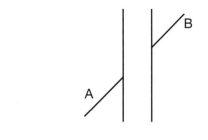

....

....

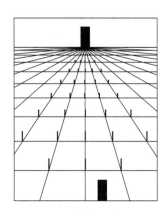

....

....

3 Our brain

3.1 Language in the brain

Read about 'Broca's area' in the brain. Draw a circle around each relative clause ('who … ' or 'which … ') and show what it describes.

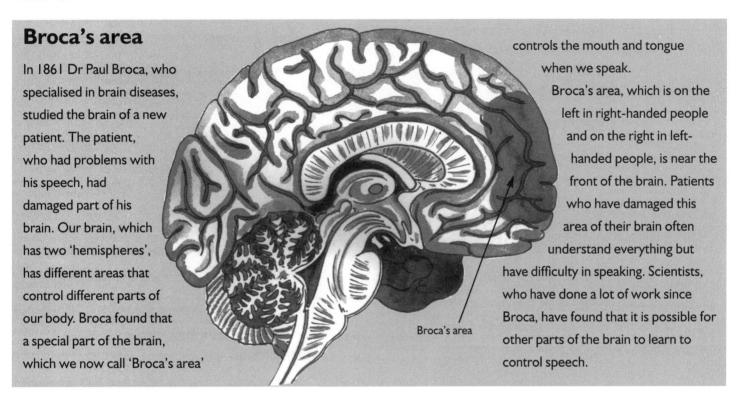

Broca's area

In 1861 Dr Paul Broca, who specialised in brain diseases, studied the brain of a new patient. The patient, who had problems with his speech, had damaged part of his brain. Our brain, which has two 'hemispheres', has different areas that control different parts of our body. Broca found that a special part of the brain, which we now call 'Broca's area' controls the mouth and tongue when we speak.

Broca's area, which is on the left in right-handed people and on the right in left-handed people, is near the front of the brain. Patients who have damaged this area of their brain often understand everything but have difficulty in speaking. Scientists, who have done a lot of work since Broca, have found that it is possible for other parts of the brain to learn to control speech.

Broca's area

3.2 One sentence from two

Make one sentence from two sentences by using a relative clause. Like this:

The human brain communicates with the body all the time. It is still a mystery for scientists.

The human brain, which is still a mystery for scientists, communicates with the body all the time.

1 The brain never sleeps. It sends and receives messages twenty-four hours a day.
2 Hundreds of years ago scientists studied the human brain. They wanted to find out if everyone's brain is the same size.
3 They discovered that an adult brain is about 2% of our body weight. It weighs about 1,400 grams.
4 The brain has about 10 billion nerve cells that carry the messages around the brain. They are called 'neurons'.
5 Neurons do not grow again. They start dying the moment we are born.

4 Don't say it clearly!

4.1 Linking words with /r/

Sometimes when we speak quickly, we link words with a small /r/ sound. Listen and say these phrases.

far away	Is the cinema far away?
four o'clock	We can meet at four o'clock.
harder and harder	School work gets harder and harder.
better at English	I'm better at English than Maths.

4.2 Linking words with /w/

We do the same thing with a small /w/ sound. Listen and say these sentences.

How are you?

Throw it in the dustbin.

Do you know if he's coming tomorrow?

20 Questions about questions
Fluency

Asking questions is an important part of our lives. In this Unit you can think about some of the questions you ask.

1 Questions about questions

1.1 Any questions

How many questions do you ask every day? 5? 50? 500? Think about yesterday and try to remember the questions you asked. Write them down, in English.

1.2 Some more questions

Look at these questions. Have you asked questions like these today or yesterday? Tick [✓] the ones you asked and add some more of your own.

2 Answers

Some questions have simple answers.

A: Is it time to get up?   B: Yes, hurry up!
A: What's for breakfast?   B: It's on the table.

Sometimes people give different answers.

A: Have you done the History homework?
B: No, not yet. I didn't have time.
C: I've done it. It was really easy.

A: What did you think of that film last night?
B: It was terrible. Tony Grey is a terrible actor.
C: It was really great. Tony Grey is brilliant.

Choose six questions from Exercise 1.2 and write down some possible answers.

Time
Is it time to get up? ☐
Am I late? ☐

....

....

....

Finding and asking for things
Where's my school bag? ☐
Have you got any money? ☐
Have you seen my English book? ☐
What's for breakfast? ☐

....

....

....

Leisure time
Did you watch the football match last night? ☐
Who do you think played best? ☐
What did you think of that film last night? ☐

....

....

....

Schoolwork
Have you done the History homework? ☐
Can I borrow your pencil? ☐
What's the answer to number 4? ☐
What mark did you get? ☐

....

....

....

3 More types of questions

There are many different types of questions – here are five different types. Look at the questions and add some more of your own.

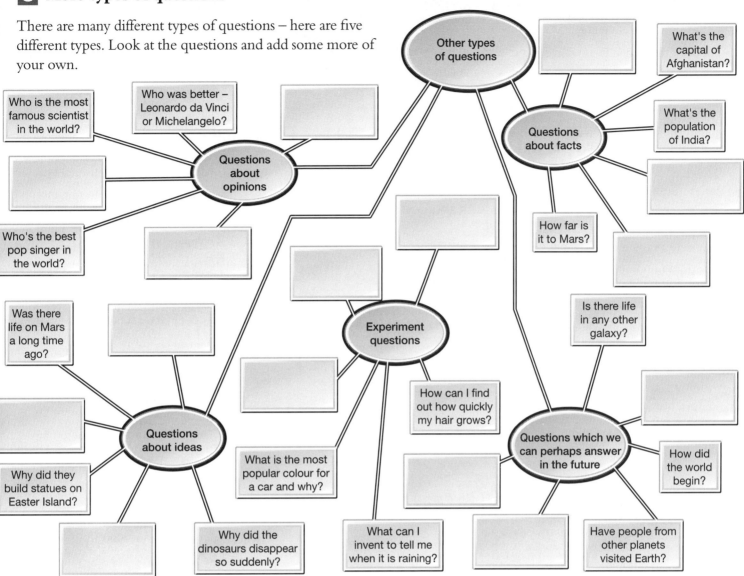

Other types of questions

What's the capital of Afghanistan?

Questions about facts

What's the population of India?

How far is it to Mars?

Is there life in any other galaxy?

Questions about opinions

Who is the most famous scientist in the world?

Who was better – Leonardo da Vinci or Michelangelo?

Who's the best pop singer in the world?

Experiment questions

Questions which we can perhaps answer in the future

How can I find out how quickly my hair grows?

How did the world begin?

Questions about ideas

Was there life on Mars a long time ago?

Why did they build statues on Easter Island?

Why did the dinosaurs disappear so suddenly?

What is the most popular colour for a car and why?

What can I invent to tell me when it is raining?

Have people from other planets visited Earth?

4 What was the question?

Asking questions helps us to invent and discover things. Look at this list. Under each item write the question that the person probably asked.

the wheel
How can I move this big animal?

writing
....

a cup
....

an engine
....

a rope
....

numbers
....

a house
....

football
....

a key
....

How can I move it?

21

Ways to reading (1): scanning

In this Unit, you can see a technique to help you with reading. 'Scanning' helps you to find information quickly. In Unit 26, you can try 'skimming' which helps you with the general meaning of a text.

1 Different texts – different reading

What have you read in the last four days? Add some more things to the brainstorm diagram.

Did you read them all in the same way? Which ones did you read fast? Which ones did you read slowly?

2 Scanning

2.1 Lists, timetables, dictionaries …

We can 'scan' lists to find information quickly. Here are some examples. Look at the texts and find:

1 a train which arrives in Castle Cary before 20.00.
2 the name 'Zelley, S. E.'.
3 the word 'peak'.
4 the page number of the article about dinosaurs.

bus

timetable

school

computer magazine 'World Network'

magazine

THINGS I HAVE READ

school text books

History

Item	
Modify	⌘M
Frame	⌘B
Step	⌘T
Duplicate	
Delete	⌘D
Group	⌘D
	⌘K
Repeat	

Bag of potatoes
tin of soup
cheese
bread
washing powder

FOOTBALL MATCHES

Duchess.
Catherine St W2.
Charing Cross tube
Stepping Out. Richard Lee
Mon - Fri 7.30pm
6pm. 8.30pm. Sat Sun
£4 - 10.

2.2 Try again

Try again! Look at the contents page of the Workbook.

1 What page does Theme F start on?
2 What is the first page of Theme A?
3 What is Unit 23 called?
4 What page is 'Ways to writing (1)' on?

2.3 Long texts

You can also scan long texts to find certain information quickly. Look for numbers, dates and key words.

There are 165 words in this text from Unit 20 of the Student's Book. How fast can you answer these questions? Look at your watch!

1 How many Native Americans are there today?
2 When did they come to America?
3 How many Americans have English ancestors?
4 How many black Americans are there today?

Native Americans –   2 million   today, about 0.8% of the population. Their ancestors came to America   Asia 40,000 years

in the 1600s, people   from Europe.

32 million Americans (about 13%) have English ancestors

are about 30 million black Americans (about 12% of the population)

2.4 Try it yourself!

Look at the rest of the text in Unit 20 of the Student's Book. It has 125 words. Find the answers to these questions as quickly as you can:

1 How many Americans have German ancestors?
2 How many Hispanics are there in America?
3 How many Asian Americans are there?

More recently, people have come to the United States from other parts of the world. Between 1820 and 1860 many people came from Germany and Ireland – about 58 million (about 23%) of Americans have German ancestors, and about 39 million (15%) have Irish ancestors. From 1860 to 1920 many more people came from other European countries including Russia, Poland, Greece, Turkey and Italy.

The USA today

Today, the fastest growing group in the United States is Hispanic. There are about 25 million Hispanics (about 9% of the population) in the United States who come from Spanish-speaking countries such as Cuba, Mexico and Puerto Rico. There are also large numbers of people from Asian countries, including China, Japan, Korea and the Philippines. In total, there are about 7.5 million Asian Americans (about 3% of the population).

A test on
Units 18–21

1 *Vocabulary*

2 *'used to'*

3 *Relative clauses (1)*

4 *Relative clauses (2)*

22

Test yourself

Here are some things you learned to do in Units 18–21. How well can you do them? Put a tick (✓) in the box.

	I can do it:	very well	OK	a little
1	Use the new words			
2	Talk about changes ('used to')			
3	Use relative causes			

Now do this test and see if you are right.

1 What's the word?

1.1 Find a pair

Join the words in List A with the correct words in List B to make a verb phrase or noun.

List A	List B
vote in	force
earn	illusion
make	place
take	saucer
a flying	sense of something
an optical	area
a labour	the light
a trick of	an election
a rural	a salary

1.2 Use the phrases

Can you complete these sentences with the correct phrase from Exercise 1.1?

1 In many countries 40% of the l............................ f............................ are women. However most of them do not e............................ a large s............................ .

2 If someone sees a f............................ s............................ , people often say it was an o............................ i............................ , caused by a t............................ o............................ t............................ l............................ .

3 We see many unusual or incomplete images every day, but our brain tries to m............................ s............................ o............................ them.

4 When people are 18 years old in many countries, they can v............................ i............................ a............................ e............................ . Elections t............................ p............................ every four or five years in many countries.

5 Young people often leave r............................ a............................ to look for work in the cities.

2 Irian Jaya, Indonesia

Irian Jaya is part of Indonesia. David Watson is talking to Efradus Basan about how life has changed there. Look at the notes on the notepad and complete the dialogue.

DAVID: Efradus, tell me about the changes in Irian Jaya.

EFRADUS: Well, Irian Jaya *used to be isolated* . Now tourists come from everywhere.

DAVID: How has life changed?

EFRADUS: Well, the first big change is our houses. In the past, many people
1 .... but now they build houses on the ground.

DAVID: And what language do you speak?

EFRADUS: Well, we ²_____ but now we are learning a new, official language.

DAVID: And how do you travel around the island?

EFRADUS: In the past, we ³_____ everywhere but now there is a big road and people ⁴_____ .

DAVID: How do people get food to eat?

EFRADUS: In the old days, we ⁵_____ but now we grow vegetables and have small farms.

DAVID: I see. And are there any schools here?

EFRADUS: Yes, there are new schools here now but I ⁶_____ .

DAVID: So what do you think about the changes?

EFRADUS: Well, we can't go back now.

Listen and check your answers.

3 Make one sentence

Make one sentence from two sentences by using a relative clause.

1 In Indonesia half the people are under twenty years old. It has a population of 180 million.

In Indonesia, which has a population of 180 million, half the people are under twenty years old.

2 Indonesia is about 4,500 kilometres wide. It has five large islands and over 300 smaller ones.

3 Many Indonesians work in the oil, gas and timber industries. They live in big cities like Jakarta, Surabaya and Bandung.

4 Indonesia has very good land to grow rice. It has 100 active volcanoes.

4 Definitions

Can you join the words to make complete definitions?

1 A cassette player	gives the meanings of words.
2 An author	is a book grows crops or has animals.
3 A camera	who gives us information.
4 An archaeologist	is a person studies things from the past.
5 An encyclopaedia	which writes books.
6 A calculator	is a machine does mathematical calculations.
7 A farmer	takes photographs.
8 A dictionary	plays recordings.

IN THE PAST
tree houses
isolated
many different languages
walk
hunt
no schools

NOW
houses on the ground
tourists
a new language
a big road
the trans–Irian highway
cars and lorries
farms
new schools

A vocabulary map (4)

Change

Write these words in the correct area of the vocabulary map. (Some words can go in two or more areas.) You can also add the meanings in your language (in the bottom half of each box). Can you add any more words that you know or any more areas to the map?

agriculture beautiful bright change cruel dark dirty female
flying saucer guess handsome independent industrialisation
industry labour force lonely make sense male message
mirage misunderstand nice pattern perception poor
recognise rural ugly urban wealthy

WORDS TO TALK ABOUT OPTICAL ILLUSIONS

flying saucer

WORDS TO TALK ABOUT THE TOWN AND COUNTRY

agriculture

female

beautiful

CHANGE

WORDS TO DESCRIBE PEOPLE

dirty

change

dark

bright

USEFUL VERBS

guess

cruel

WORDS TO TALK ABOUT OUR BRAIN

FOCUS ON
The news
Topic and language
23

1 *Vocabulary*

1 What's the word?

1.1 Odd one out

One word in each line is different from the other words. Which one? Give a reason. For example:

1 reporter   investigate   journalist

'Investigate' is different because 'reporter' and 'journalist' are people.

2 report   channel   story

3 altitude   top   peak

4 swimming   football   economics

5 crime   science   serious

6 letter   envelope   questionnaire

7 sickness   injury   recovery

8 tragic   sharp   sad

9 order   sequence   teenager

10 programme   advertisement   poster

1.2 A puzzle

Write your answers from Exercise 1.1 in the correct space in the puzzle.
(Be careful with the numbers!)

Can you make a word with the letters in the squares like this:

Clue: Political stories about the
.... usually come first on the news.

1.3 Your puzzle

Make an 'odd one out' puzzle like this for your class. Find some words in the wordlist.

2 Can you believe the news?

2.1 What do they say?

These students are talking about the news. Which students say that you can believe the news? Which students say that you can't?

Write the letters in two columns.

We can believe the news   We can't believe the news

a I think the advertisers tell the TV companies what to put in the news.

b The TV companies ar all independent. They on tell us what happens.

c The news reports the facts, doesn't it?

d They make the news sound exciting so that we'll watch it more often.

e It's the same information as in the newspapers so it must be true.

f I think the government tells the TV companies what to say.

g If the news wasn't true, we would soon find out the truth.

h You never hear the full facts on the TV news – the stories are too short.

i Sometimes the reporters make things up just to have a good story.

j TV cameras can't lie! They always tell the truth.

2.2 What do you think?

What do you think about the news? Ask your friends and family what they think and write a few sentences.

3 Don't say it clearly!

3.1 Listen to the silence

Many words have letters which are silent. Listen to these words and put a circle around the silent letters.

colum(n)   half   often   talk
listen   know   would

3.2 Say the sentences

Now listen and say these sentences. Put a circle around the silent letters in the underlined words.

Last Wednesday, two men climbed a mountain in India. They did it in 24 hours. They do it every autumn. Why? Their answer is very simple: they love climbing mountains!

4 Question tags

4.1 Match the question tag

Join the two parts of the sentence.

1 She isn't in Class 5, …   a … isn't there?

2 All the students in this class   b … wasn't it?
  have finished Book 2, …

3 There's still a war in Africa, …   c … isn't it?

4 That was a terrible air crash, …   d … wasn't he?

5 Teachers should wear   e … haven't they?
  a uniform, too, …

6 The scientist who discovered   f … shouldn't they?
  penicillin was Scottish, …

7 It's too hot to work today, …   g … is she?

🔲 Listen and check your answers.

4.2 Checking or asking?

🔲 Listen to the sentences again. Are the speakers checking something or are they sure? Write 'C' and draw an arrow like this ⤵ or 'S' and draw an arrow like this ⤴ .

5 Talk to Maggi

🔲 Write your answers to Maggi's questions. Then talk to her on the cassette.

MAGGI: Hi! What's happening in your part of the world this week?

YOU: ....

....

MAGGI: I like listening to the news. What's the most amazing news story you have ever heard?

YOU: ....

....

MAGGI: Oh! Last month I heard that scientists think there was life on Mars. What do you think about that?

YOU: ....

....

MAGGI: I like the news stories about discoveries – when they find old dinosaur bones or go inside a pyramid, for example. What kind of news stories do you like best?

YOU: ....

....

MAGGI: Oh, do you? I like knowing about famous people too. Do you like those stories?

YOU: ....

....

MAGGI: I think I'd like to be a news reporter. What kind of job do you want to do?

YOU: ....

....

MAGGI: Oh! I've got to go now. It was nice talking to you. Bye!

YOU: ....

....

Vocabulary;
reading; Present
passive;
intonation
of question forms

1 *Vocabulary*

2 *Present passive*

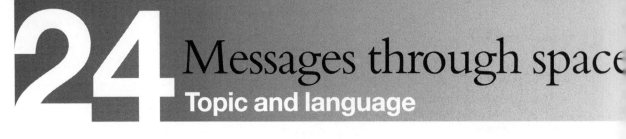

24 Messages through space
Topic and language

1 Definitions

1.1 Definition puzzle

Read the definition and find the word in the puzzle.

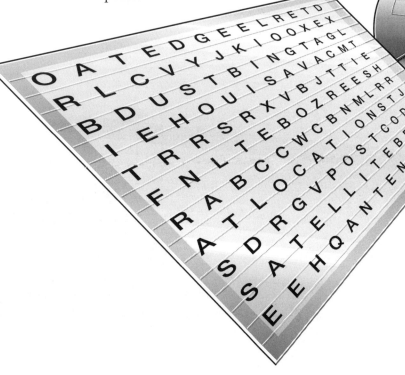

n. = noun   *v.* = verb   *adj.* = adjective
pl. = plural

1 *n.* a machine put in orbit around the Earth:
   s..

2 *n.* a place where we put household rubbish:
   d..

3 *n.pl.* aerials on a satellite:
   a..

4 *n.* some letters or numbers in a postal
   address: p..

5 *v.* and *n.* to move round the earth in a fixed
   path: o..

6 *v.* to turn on an axis: r..

7 *adj.* precise, correct: e..

8 *n.* a position or place: l..

1.2 Example sentences

Complete these example sentences with one
of the words from the puzzle.

1 If you put the .... with the
   address on an envelope, the letter will arrive
   quicker.

2 Some families now have four
   .... in different colours:
   one for paper, one for tins, one for glass and
   one for rubbish.

3 Satellites are like insects: they have
   .... to pick up sound
   waves.

4 Satellites continue to ....
   the Earth after they have broken down.

5 The Earth .... on its axis
   every 23 hours, 56 minutes and 4 seconds.

6 .... are used for many
   modern means of communication such as
   radio and cellular phones.

7 No one knows the ....
   number of satellites in space.

8 Communications satellites have a fixed
   .... in space.

2 Rules, processes and actions

2.1 Types of sentences

In your Student's Book you saw that the Passive is often used in English when:

a the action is more important than who does it.

b you describe a process.

c you write a rule.

Read these sentences and write a, b or c beside each one.

1 Two hundred umbrellas are left in London taxis every day.
2 More satellites are sent into orbit every day.
3 Personal stereos are forbidden in the classroom.
4 First, the small trees are cleared and then the bigger trees are cut down.
5 Radio waves are transmitted into space and then 'reflected' by satellites.
6 Portuguese is spoken in Brazil.
7 No food or drink is allowed in the museum.
8 Skating is forbidden in the park.

2.2 A telephone call

Read about the different stages in a telephone call and fill in the flow chart.

When we make a phone call, first we dial the numbers on the telephone. Each time we press or dial a number, a signal is transmitted. These signals are received by automatic equipment in the exchange. The call is then connected and the other telephone starts to ring. When you speak into the telephone, the sound of your voice is changed into electrical signals by the microphone inside. These signals are sent to the telephone at the other end. There they are changed back into sound by the receiver.

1 We dial the numbers.
2
3 Signals are received by automatic equipment.
4
5
6
7 Signals are sent to the other telephone.
8

2.3 How do mobile phones work?

Look at the flow chart and describe the process.

There is a small transmitter and receiver in a mobile phone. When we make a call with a mobile phone ...

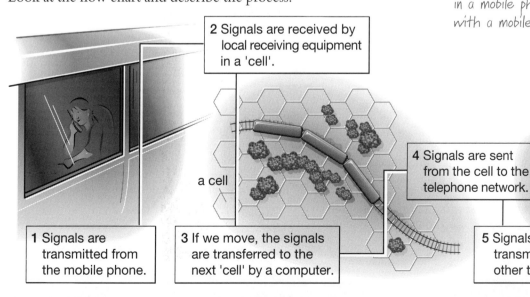

2 Signals are received by local receiving equipment in a 'cell'.

4 Signals are sent from the cell to the telephone network.

a cell

1 Signals are transmitted from the mobile phone.

3 If we move, the signals are transferred to the next 'cell' by a computer.

5 Signals are transmitted to the other telephone.

3 *Intonation of questions*

4 *Writing and speaking*

3 Say it clearly!

3.1 Sometimes questions go up …

When we ask questions in English our voice can go up or down at the end. Our voice goes UP when we ask a 'yes/no' question.

🔲 Listen and say the questions.

A: Do you watch TV every day?
B: Yes, I do!

A: Do you like football?
B: No, I hate it!

A: Have you seen this video before?
B: Yes, I saw it last week.

A: Did you go to the cinema last night?
B: No, I didn't. I stayed at home.

3.2 … and sometimes questions go down

Our voice goes DOWN when we ask an 'information question' (Where? What? How? Why? When? How long?).

🔲 Listen and say the sentences.

I like your skates. Where did you buy them?

I went to the cinema last night. What did you do?

That's a brilliant model. When did you make it?

Why don't you eat meat?

3.3 Up or down?

Read these questions. Draw an arrow like this ⌐ or like this ⌐ next to each one.

Do you live near school?
Where do you live?
Why don't you catch the bus?
Do you walk to school?
What's your favourite group?
Do you like folk music?
When did you go to America?
Have you been to New York?
What do you usually do at weekends?
Do you want to go swimming on Saturday?
What class are you in?

🔲 Listen and check your answers. The UP questions come first on the cassette.

4 Talk to Lewis

🔲 Write your answers to Lewis' questions. Then talk to him on the cassette.

LEWIS: Hi! We're doing a survey at school about television and radio. Can you help me?

YOU: ....

LEWIS: Thanks! My first question is what kinds of programmes do you listen to on the radio?

YOU: ....
....
....

LEWIS: OK. Thanks. Next, when you listen to music is it on the radio, on a cassette, on a CD or on a record?

YOU: ....

LEWIS: Mmm. I like cassettes because I share them with my friends and CDs are quite expensive. Now then, television. What kinds of TV programmes do you like best?

YOU: ....
....
....
....

LEWIS: Oh, do you? How often do you watch TV?

YOU: ....

LEWIS: Thanks. My next question is: have you got a radio, a TV, a video, cassette or CD player in your bedroom?

YOU: ....
....

LEWIS: I've got a cassette player and radio in my bedroom. I listen to music when I'm doing my homework. Do you listen to music then?

YOU: ....

LEWIS: Well, thanks for answering my questions. Talk to you soon! Bye!

YOU: ....

Labyrinths are amazing!

Fluency

In this Unit you can learn to draw labyrinths. Follow the instructions. You need a pencil and a rubber because everyone makes mistakes the first time.

1 The three-circuit labyrinth

1.1 A left-handed labyrinth

This is called a left-handed labyrinth because when you walk in, you have to turn left.

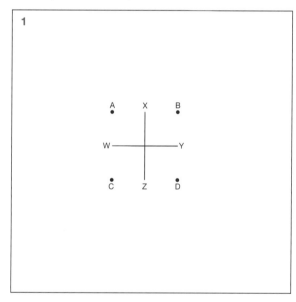

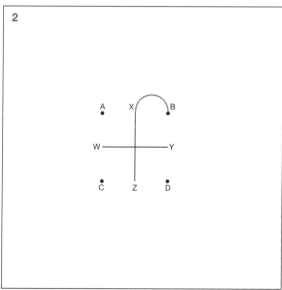

A three-circuit labyrinth

1 First, draw a cross and four dots.

2 Now, start at the top of the cross. Put your pencil at X and draw a loop – a curved line – to B.

2 Now move to the dot in the top left. Put your pencil on A and draw a loop to Y. Make sure that the loop goes outside the first one.

3 Now move your pencil across the line from Y to W. Draw a loop outside the first and second lines from W all the way round to D.

4 Now move your pencil to the dot in the bottom left – to C. Draw a loop all the way round the outside of all the other loops to Z.

5 Now you can label your labyrinth.

– The part in the centre is called 'the goal'.

– The entrance is called 'the mouth'.

– The lines you have drawn are called 'walls'.

– The spaces are called 'paths'.

Put numbers on the paths. Number 1 is the outside path from the mouth, then number 2, then number 3 nearest the goal.

Your labyrinth is finished. First, go round the labyrinth with your finger from the mouth to the goal and then with your pencil.

1.2 A right-handed labyrinth

You can use the same cross and dots pattern but draw a right-handed labyrinth.

Here are the first two instructions. Draw the labyrinth and write the other instructions.

1 Start at the top of the cross. Put your pencil at X and draw a loop – a curved line – to A.

2 Now move to the dot in the top right square. Put your pencil on B and draw a loop to W. Make sure that the loop goes outside the first one.

3 ....

   ....

4 ....

   ....

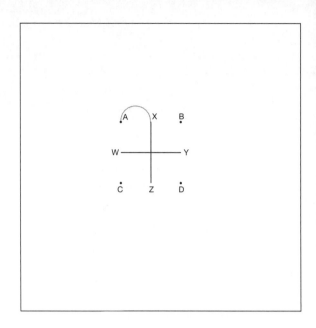

2 The seven-circuit labyrinth

This is the most common type of labyrinth.

Follow the first part of the instructions and draw the seven-circuit left-handed labyrinth.

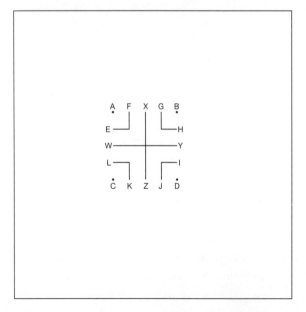

1 Put your pencil on X. Draw a curved line to G.

2 Lift up your pencil and move to the top left corner. Put your pencil on F. Draw a loop around to B. Make sure you go outside the first loop.

3 Lift up your pencil and move to the dot in the top left-hand corner – A. Put your pencil on A. Draw a loop around to the end of the line – H – outside the other loops.

4 Now move back to the left-hand side of the diagram and put your pencil on E. Draw a loop around the other lines to Y.

5 Go back to the left again and put your pencil on W. Draw another loop – this time to I.

Now you should have the system in your mind. Write the next three stages.

6 ....

   ....

7 ....

   ....

8 ....

   ....

Ways to reading (2): skimming

In this Unit you can see some more techniques to help with reading. You can use these techniques when you are reading in English or in your language.

1 Make reading easier!

1.1 First and last paragraphs

When you read a long text, you often don't have to read all of it. Sometimes you just want to find out the main ideas. You can make reading easier if you do this:

a Read the title first
b Read the first and last paragraphs
c Read the headings
Now think! What will the text say?

Try with this text.

Which of these sentences do you think are in the missing text? Write 'P' (probably) or 'DN' (definitely not) next to each sentence.

1 Countries around the world united to form The World Heritage Organisation in 1972.
2 Everybody wants to have their own car.
3 There are many different ideas about how to solve the problem of vandalism.
4 There is no point in repairing old buildings.
5 Children like playing with their grandparents.
6 At some sites, governments have built high fences to protect the site from vandals.

Now check your answers. Look at the text in Unit 28 in your Student's Book.

HOW CAN WE LOOK AFTER THE PAST?

Our children and grandchildren may not have a chance to visit many of the most famous places around the world. War, weather, age, traffic and pollution damage these famous places. There is a need for constant renovation. But looking after these places often costs more than one country can afford.

The World Heritage Organisation

Vandalism: one of the biggest problems

Other experts say that the best solution is education. If people learned to respect history, they would not destroy or damage it. They would also want to spend money to look after old places. For this reason, The World Heritage Organisation helps to spread information about the value of historic sites.

1.2 Try again!

Look at Unit 29 of your Student's Book. Look at the text about the Giant's Causeway and do this:

a Read the titles
b Look at the pictures
c Read from 'The Giant's Causeway' to 'Finn MacCool' and from 'Geologists say' to the end

Now write down what other information you think will be in the text. Read the text and check your ideas!

Now read the text about the Galapagos Islands from 'The Galapagos Islands' to 'are only found here' and from 'Some tortoises' to the end. Can you guess what other information is in the text?

2 Make reading easier! First and last sentences

2.1 The main idea

Sometimes we can get the main idea by reading the first two sentences or the last two sentences of a paragraph. Read these sentences.

Great Zimbabwe, Zimbabwe

In 1871 Karl Mauch, a German, discovered huge stone walls in Zimbabwe, Africa. The walls covered 25 hectares around what is now called 'Great

archaeologists. They think the Great Enclosure was built about 1,000 years ago.

Do you think the following information is in the complete paragraph? Put a tick (✓) if you think 'Yes' and put a cross (✗) if you think 'No'.

a more information about what Great Zimbabwe was
b more about the life of Karl Mauch
c information about the Great Enclosure
d information about the climate in Africa
e information about life in 1871

Now look at Unit 28 in your Student's Book and check your answers.

2.2 Try again!

Read these sentences and write down what you think is in the rest of each paragraph. Then check in Unit 28 of your Student's Book.

Pueblo Bonito, New Mexico, USA

One thousand years ago, in the desert of the Chaco Canyon, the Anasazi people built nine multi-storey buildings called 'Great Houses'. They used stone for the walls and wood for the floors, doors and roofs.

Easter Island, Chile

Perhaps they used all the natural resources on the island. There are many unanswered questions about Easter Island.

Test yourself 27

Here are some things you learned to do in
Units 23 – 26. How well can you do them?
Put a tick (✓)
in the box.

	I can do it:	*very well*	*OK*	*a little*
1	Use new words			
2	Use question tags			
3	Talk about sequences (present passive)			

Now do this test and see if you are right.

1 Orbit puzzle

Read the clues and write the words in the
puzzle. The last letter of the first word is the
first letter of the next word.

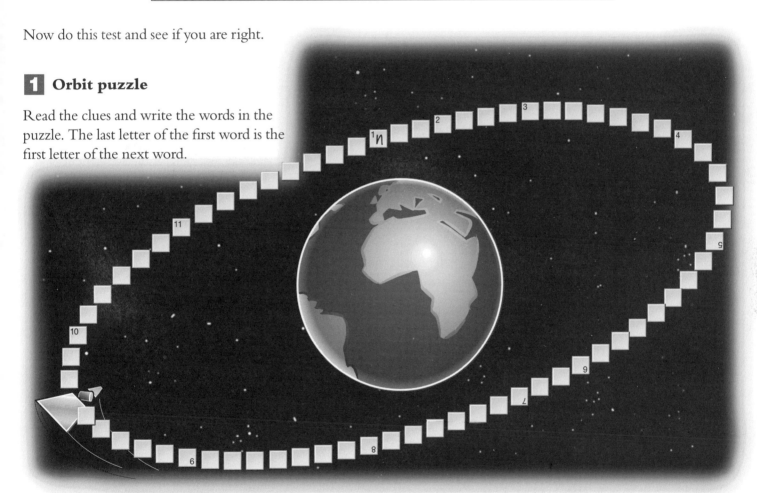

1 These programmes are usually on the radio
  every hour.

2 Football, swimming and tennis are all types
  of ....

3 Somebody aged 13–19 is a ....

4 A journalist writes a .... for a newspaper.

5 To move something from one place to
  another.

6 When two people are in a race, the referee
  has to .... them to see who is the fastest.

7 You need one if you want to send a letter.

8 A school subject about money, banks
  and trade.

9 A machine that helps us to send messages to
  the other side of the world.

10 Part of something, for example a short part
   from a story.

11 A machine that people watch a lot!

2 What can you say?

Write sentences with question tags for these situations. Show if your voice goes up or down.

1 You're not sure if there is a Maths exam on Thursday. You ask someone.

   There's a Maths exam on Thursday,
   isn't there?

2 You think the new History teacher is very nice.

3 You suggest to your friend that you can play handball this afternoon.

4 You are almost certain that Mount Kilimanjaro is in Kenya. You ask your teacher.

5 You don't think your friend has seen the film *Back to the Future*. Check.

6 You are not sure how much a cinema ticket costs. You think it costs £4 so you ask your friend.

3 How do they develop photographs?

Read about how they develop photographs. Can you complete the sentences with the correct phrase?

are done   is done   is dried   is inserted   is put
is placed   is put   is removed   is washed
is washed and dried

▭ Listen and check your answers.

DEVELOPING *and* PRINTING PHOTOGRAPHS

There are two main steps in producing photographs: developing and printing. Each step [1] .... *in a dark place.*

1 Developing the negatives

First, the film [2] .... from its case.

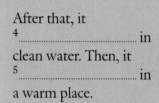

Next, it [3] .... into different chemicals. These develop it, 'stop it' and 'fix it' so that the image does not change.

After that, it [4] .... in clean water. Then, it [5] .... in a warm place.

2 Printing the photographs

To make a print, the negative [6] .... in an 'enlarger'. This projects the image at special photographic paper.

Then, the photographic paper [7] .... into chemicals to develop it and fix it. Finally, it [8] ....

In photographic laboratories, this process is done in big machines. Film [9] .... at one end, and prints come out at the other end. Developing, fixing, washing and drying [10] .... automatically inside the machine.

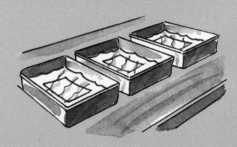

A vocabulary map (5)

Messages through space

Write these words in the correct area of the
vocabulary map. (Some words can go in two or
more areas.) You can also add the meanings in
your language (in the bottom half of each box).
Can you add any more words that you know or
any more areas to the map?

altitude antennae broadcasts bulletins channel crash
crime daily deliver economics envelope foreign news
home news location orbit politics postcode rotate
satellite to be missing tragic transport weather forecast

THEME F

Vocabulary;
intonation:
prepositions and
stress; second
conditional

1 *Vocabulary
and
reading*

2 *Prepositions
and
stress*

3 *Second
conditional*

28 FOCUS ON
Our heritage
Topic and language

1 'A rose-red city, half as old as time'

There are eight words hidden in the picture. Can you find them? Write the correct word in each space in the text.

The city of Petra in Jordan was built about 2,500 years ago by people called the Nabataeans. Many of the buildings were
¹ _____ – many metres high.
They were also very ² _____
because they were ³ _____ from the red sandstone and they shone like jewels in the sun.

Today, the city is in ruins and it is quiet except for tourists and tourist ⁴ _____ , but for many years Petra was an important trade centre. Camels, horses and donkeys used to
⁵ _____ spices, perfumes and cloth from Arabia to the Mediterranean. Traders used to stop at Petra for water which came from the Wadi Musa well. Soldiers used to
⁶ _____ the traders from attack.

In 106 AD the Romans captured the city. Soldiers
⁷ _____ buildings and later the desert sands came into the city and
⁸ _____ the streets and the houses. Now, very little remains of this romantic 'rose-red' city.

2 Say it clearly!

2.1 Prepositions and questions

Prepositions are usually 'weak' in English. Listen.

I was talking to /tə/ Jack yesterday.
He comes from /frəm/ New York.

But prepositions at the end of a question are 'strong'. Listen.

Who were you talking TO?
Where does he come FROM?

Say these questions. Stress the preposition.

1 What do you want that for?
2 What is she looking at?
3 Who is the letter from?
4 If you can't spell the word look it up.
5 What time did they get up?
6 Come on! Hurry up!

2.2 Stress for contrast

🎙️ You also stress prepositions if they are important to the meaning of the sentence, or for contrast. Listen.

Is this letter TO Tom or FROM him?
Are the students IN the school or OUTSIDE it?

Say these sentences. Stress the prepositions.

1 Is this lift going up or down?
2 Is the cassette player on or off?
3 Let's meet outside the cinema, not inside it.
4 Are the books on the table or under it?

2.3 Strong or weak?

🎙️ Listen to these sentences. Write 'W' if the preposition is weak (not stressed) and 'S' if the preposition is strong (stressed).

1 Traders stopped for water in Petra. ☐
2 Is Petra on the coast or in the centre of Jordan? ☐
3 I'd love to go to Jordan. ☐
4 I'd never heard of Petra before. ☐
5 Petra is made of red sandstone. ☐
6 It's empty except for tourists. ☐
7 What are you listening to? ☐
8 Who are you talking to? ☐

3 Suggestions

3.1 What do they think?

These students are thinking of different ways they can improve their school. Match the two parts of the suggestions.

1. If we had a clean water fountain …
2. If the school meals were cheaper …
3. If we had more sports lessons …
4. If we didn't have so much homework …
5. If we had a place to put our bicycles …
6. If we had an 'English evening' concert …
7. If we had a lost property office …

a … we wouldn't be so tired.
b … our parents would hear all our English songs.
c … we wouldn't buy fizzy drinks.
d … we would ride our bikes to school.

e … we wouldn't bring sandwiches.
f … we would be able to find our things.
g … we would have a better football team.

3.2 What would happen if …?

Complete these sentences with your ideas.
Use 'would' and your imagination!

1 If it didn't rain again …
   all the rivers would be dry.
   The grass would be brown.
   We would have no water.

2 If Martians landed on Earth …

3 If everyone wore the same clothes …

4 If there were no football teams …

5 If the government banned cars completely …

6 If you found a spider in your lunch …

3.3 What would you do if …?

Answer the questions with your own ideas.

1 What would you do if you were
  President/Prime Minister of your country?

2 Where would you go if you won a 'round the
  world' ticket?

3 What would you say if you met your favourite
  pop star, film star or sports person?

4 Where would you live if you had a choice?

5 How would you change your town if you had a
  lot of money?

4 Talk to Lewis

📟 Look at the picture and write your
answers to Lewis' questions. Then talk to him
on the cassette.

LEWIS: Hi! Listen, can you help me with my
        homework?

YOU: ....

LEWIS: Well, there's a really old castle in our town.
        Have you got any old buildings in your
        town?

YOU: ....
        ....

LEWIS: Oh. Well, the castle
        here is in a terrible
        condition. We have
        to think of some
        ideas about how we
        can improve it. Can
        you think of any
        ideas?

YOU: ....
        ....

LEWIS: Mmm. What can we do about the roof?

YOU: ....

LEWIS: That's an idea. I thought we could put
        lights near the castle. Do you think that's a
        good idea?

YOU: ....
        ....

LEWIS: What can we do about the problem with
        the rubbish everywhere?

YOU: ....
        ....

LEWIS: Yes, I thought that, too! Well, I must think
        of some more ideas! Thanks for your help.
        Bye!

Natural wonders 29
Topic and language

1 Lake Vanda

1.1 Noun, verb or adjective?

First read through the text quickly. Decide what kind of word is missing in each gap – noun, verb or adjective. Write 'N', 'V' or 'A'.

Lake Vanda, which is 75 metres [1].............................., is in a polar region in a very [2]........................... part of the world called the Dry Valleys in Antarctica. There hasn't been any rain there for two million years. It is one of the most [3].. lakes in the world with three [4].................................. features. Firstly, the Onyx river which [5]........................... into it flows *from* the sea not *into* it. Secondly, the lake has fresh water at the [6]........................... but salty water underneath. Thirdly, when the temperature [7]............................... in the winter there are 4 metres of [8]....................... at the top but the water below has a [9]........................... temperature of 25 °C.

Lake Vanda, Antarctica

How does it happen?

Firstly, the water in the Onyx river comes from the melting ice from a [10].. on the coast. The force of the ice causes the river to run inland. Secondly, the heat of the sun causes the surface water to [11].. . Then the salt crystals [12]................................. to the bottom of the lake. Thirdly, the ice on the surface [13]............................. a greenhouse effect which [14]................................ the water below.

1.2 An iceberg puzzle

Now complete the gaps with a word from the iceberg.

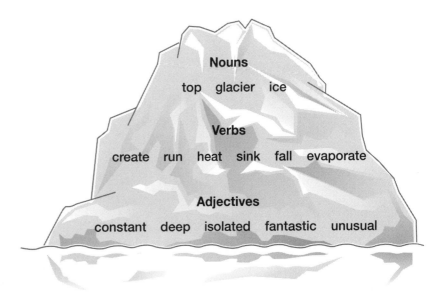

Nouns
top   glacier   ice

Verbs
create   run   heat   sink   fall   evaporate

Adjectives
constant   deep   isolated   fantastic   unusual

2 It will probably happen …

2.1 'If + not'

'Unless' means 'if + not'. Look:

<u>If we don't</u> protect our environment, many animals will disappear.

<u>Unless</u> we protect our environment, many animals will disappear.

Join the two parts of the sentence.

1 Unless we protect rare animals, …

2 Unless we share the costs, …

3 Unless we do something now, …

4 Unless we use security guards, …

a … poorer countries will not be able to protect their heritage.

b … it will be too late.

c … vandals will damage our old buildings.

d … they will disappear.

2.2 What will happen?

Complete these sentences with your own words. Remember to use 'will' or 'won't' in the second phrase.

1 Unless I make a list of the new words, …

....

2 Unless I go to bed early, …

....

3 Unless I revise for the test, …

....

4 Unless I save some of my pocket money, …

....

5 Unless I go home now, …

....

3 Egypt

Complete the text with the correct form of the Past passive. You can use these verbs.

build call pour use push send put

make repeat

How and why were the pyramids built?

In Egypt the kings and queens
¹ _____ *were called* _____ 'Pharaohs'. All
the pyramids ² .... as
tombs for the pharaohs, but the plans for
the pyramid ³ ....
while the pharaoh was alive. Only very
simple tools ⁴ .... to
construct the pyramids. Teams of slaves and
prisoners ⁵ .... into
the desert to get the stone. The workers
used blocks of wood to cut the stone. They
used a special technique to do this. The
wood ⁶ .... into a
hole in the stone and then water
⁷ .... onto the wood.
When the wood was wet it expanded. Often
this process ⁸ ....
many times before the stone broke. Then
the stones ⁹ .... to
the pyramid on logs.

Stonehenge, England

4 **Talk to Maggi**

Write your answers to Maggi's questions. Then talk to her on the cassette.

MAGGI: Hi! It was great today. We had History. It's my favourite subject. What subject do you like best?

YOU: ....

MAGGI: What was your most interesting lesson this week?

YOU: ....
....

MAGGI: Oh, really. Well, we learned about how they made buildings thousands of years ago. What did you do in your lesson?

YOU: ....
....
....

MAGGI: Oh. Well, we learned about Stonehenge. It's a very old site with enormous stones in England. Have you got anything big and old like that in your country?

YOU: ....
....

MAGGI: I see. We're going to watch a video about how they made Stonehenge tomorrow. Do you watch many videos at your school?

YOU: ....
....

MAGGI: Well, the stones at Stonehenge are very big. They are all standing in a circle. Do you know how they moved the stones?

YOU: ....
....
....

MAGGI: Some people think they put them on logs and rolled them. I'm not sure. Anyway, I'm going to read some more about Stonehenge now. What are you going to do?

YOU: ....
....

MAGGI: Oh, that sounds good too. Talk to you soon. Bye!

YOU: ....

30 The minotaur
Fluency

1 The minotaur

Read one of the famous Greek legends about the minotaur – a dangerous beast that was half man and half bull. You can also find out why today Greeks call the sea between Greece and Turkey the 'Aegean Sea'.

The story is on the cassette.

The minotaur

Poseidon's present

A long time ago, a young man called Minos became the King of Crete. He knew that the god of the sea, Poseidon, had helped other kings before, so he went to ask Poseidon for help.

'Poseidon,' he said, 'I want to give the gods a present so that they will help me to be a good king.'

'You're a good and kind man, Minos, so I'll help you,' said Poseidon. 'I'll give you one of my best bulls to give to the gods. They will be pleased with that.'

Immediately, a beautiful white bull came running out of the sea. It was so perfect that King Minos did not want to kill it so he killed another bull instead and gave it as a present to the gods. Poseidon knew what had happened and became very angry.

The minotaur

'A horrible monster will come from this bull,' Poseidon said to King Minos, 'and there will be trouble all through your country.'

Poseidon was right. A horrible monster called the minotaur came from the bull. The minotaur was half man and half bull. It killed people and ran through the country, terrifying everyone.

King Minos went to find Daedalus. Daedalus was an inventor and an architect who had invented many strange new things which had helped people before. 'Daedalus, can you help me? What can we do about this horrible monster, the minotaur? It's killing people all over the island.'

Daedalus thought for a while and replied, 'I'll build a labyrinth and we can put the minotaur in the centre so it won't be able to get out.'

'That's an excellent idea,' replied King Minos, 'and when I have prisoners I will send them into the labyrinth for the minotaur to eat.'

Theseus and the minotaur

Many years before this, King Minos had had a war with King Aegeus of Athens. Minos defeated Aegeus, so at the end of the war, Minos said, 'You have lost the war and so every year you must send seven young men and seven young women to Crete as our prisoners. If you do not do this, there will be another war.' The King of Athens had to agree to this, and now each year King Minos sent the prisoners into the labyrinth for the minotaur to eat.

Now, King Aegeus had a son called Theseus. Theseus wanted to stop the agreement with Minos so he asked his father if he could go to Crete. 'Please, father,' said Theseus, 'send me to Crete and I can kill the minotaur.' The king knew that his son was strong and brave and finally agreed to let him go. He told Theseus to fly a white flag from his ship as he returned, so that he would know that he had killed the minotaur.

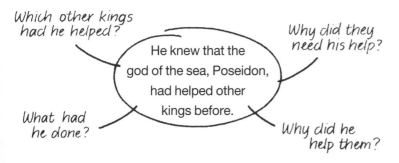

Daedalus' string

When Theseus arrived on Crete, Ariadne, one of Minos' daughters, fell in love with him. She didn't want Theseus to go into the labyrinth because she knew that the minotaur would kill him. She ran to Daedalus and asked for help.

'Please help me, Daedalus. Theseus is going into the labyrinth tomorrow. What can we do?'

Daedalus gave her some string and said, 'Tell Theseus to tie this string at the entrance to the labyrinth. If he goes quietly into the labyrinth, he will be able to kill the minotaur while it is asleep and then he can follow the string to escape from the labyrinth.'

Theseus took the string into the labyrinth and killed the minotaur. Then, following the string, he came out from the labyrinth with the other prisoners.

Tired, Theseus sailed back towards Athens, but he forgot to fly a white flag from his ship. His father, King Aegeus, saw Theseus' ship coming back with a black flag and, thinking that his son had died in the labyrinth, he threw himself into the sea – which is why, today, the Greeks call it the 'Aegean Sea'.

2 A story within a story

2.1 Questions and answers

In the legend, there are some events without a lot of detail. You can ask yourself some questions about them. Look:

> Which other kings had he helped?
>
> He knew that the god of the sea, Poseidon, had helped other kings before.
>
> Why did they need his help?
>
> What had he done?
>
> Why did he help them?

Read the story again. Find another event that doesn't have a lot of detail and write some questions about it.

2.2 Pen to paper

Look at your questions from Exercise 2.1. You can use your questions to help you write another part of the story. Like this:

a Add some more questions if you can.

b Next, make some notes about your answers to each question.

c Number your answers in the order you want them.

d Then, use your answers to write your story.

e Check your work – think about spelling, grammar and vocabulary.

f Write it out again. You can add maps or drawings.

31
Ways to speaking and listening (2)

In this Unit you can see some techniques to help with speaking and listening in English or in your language.

1 Ways to check that you understand someone

1.1 Do I understand them?

Here are some ways to check that you understand someone. Have you tried them before? Can you add some of your own ideas?

1.2 Listen!

Listen to some examples. Notice what person B says.

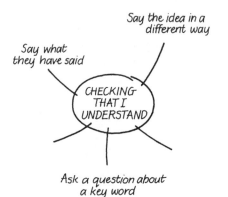

Say what they have said

Say the idea in a different way

CHECKING THAT I UNDERSTAND

Ask a question about a key word

Example 1: Say the idea in a different way.

A: Well, I think we should think about different ways to use our old things so that we don't waste the world's valuable resources. This will save money and energy.

B: So, you think we can recycle a lot of things?

A: Yes, that's right.

Example 2: Ask a question about a key word.

A: So, today we are going to learn more about photosynthesis in plants and how it is important for the Earth's climate.

B: Can you explain 'photosynthesis' again, please?

A: Yes, plants use sunlight to …

Example 3: Say what they have said.

A: So, if you want to use this computer, you first need to switch it on here. Then, you have to choose the program you want from the menu and press 'Enter'.

B: OK, so first I switch it on here and then I choose a program and press this key.

A: Yes, that's right. And then you …

1.3 Now you try!

Practise each technique. Record some sentences from a text in the Student's Book. Leave some space for you to speak after each one. Play the cassette back and say a reply to check that you understand.

2 Ways to check they understand you

2.1 Do they understand me?

Here are some ways you can use to check that people understand you. Can you add some of your own ideas?

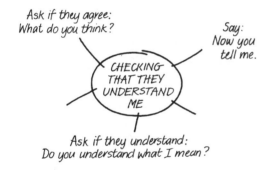

Ask if they agree:
What do you think?

Say:
Now you tell me.

CHECKING THAT THEY UNDERSTAND ME

Ask if they understand:
Do you understand what I mean?

2.2 Listen!

▭ Listen to some examples.

Example 1: Do you understand what I mean?
I don't understand this computer. I want to save my work but each time I press this key I lose it all! The computer goes 'beep!' and then 'clonk!' and it all disappears. Do you understand what I mean?

Example 2: Can you remember?
To make a pancake, put 100 grams of flour in a bowl. Make a well in the centre. Break the egg and put it in the well. Pour in the milk quite slowly and whisk hard until the mixture is very smooth. Heat some oil in the pan and put in enough mixture to cover the pan. Cook for about four minutes. Your turn! Can you remember what to do? Tell me.

Example 3: Ask if they agree: What do you think?
Yesterday, I read this article about the mystery of the Bermuda Triangle. Lots of people think there is a magic force there that makes planes and ships crash. What do you think?

2.3 Now you try!

Look at this list of topics. Write a few sentences about each one. Use a different 'checking' technique for each topic. Record yourself on a cassette.

1 Instructions for playing a game

2 Your opinion about a new film

3 Your ideas about how to improve television programmes in your country

Revision of Units
28–31

1 *Vocabulary*

2 *'unless'*

3 *Second
conditional*

4 *Past passive*

32

Revision and evaluation

Here are some things you learned to do in Units 28–31. How well can you do them? Put a tick (✓) in the box.

Now choose some of these sections to revise and practise.

	I can do it:	*very well*	*OK*	*a little*
1	Use the new words			
2	Use 'unless'			
3	Talk about imaginary events (second conditional)			
4	Make sentences with the Past passive			

1 The words you met

1.1 Word pairs

Here are some of the words you saw in Units 28–31. The first word in each set is sometimes used with one of the words a–d. Can you match them? For example:

			a		**b**		**c**		**d**	
1	*endangered*		a	causeway	b	myth	c	species	d	giant
2	*natural*		a	culture	b	resources	c	legend	d	volcano
3	*historic*		a	language	b	copy	c	column	d	site
4	*wide*		a	gaps	b	designs	c	movements	d	rock formations
5	*urgent*		a	place	b	legend	c	help	d	future
6	*preserve*		a	a design	b	our history	c	a hut	d	a mystery
7	*geometric*		a	religion	b	design	c	characteristic	d	influence

1.2 Complete the sentences

Now choose the correct word pair for each sentence.

a In the Great Rift Valley there are .... over 60 metres across.

b The columns of the Giant's Causeway in Northern Ireland seem to have a ....

c Machu Picchu, in Peru, is an example of an ....

d People probably abandoned Easter Island because they used all the ....

e If we want future generations to learn about their past, we have to ....

f The giant tortoises on the Galapagos Islands are an example of an ....

g Many other animals need .... so that they can survive.

2 There will be trouble unless ...

Think of six things you must do (today, tomorrow or next week) and write about what will happen if you don't do them. For example:

Unless I go to bed now, I will wake up too late tomorrow morning.

3 Problems in the woods

Some students had a meeting to brainstorm some ideas about how to protect a wood and its animals. Read the notes and write a sentence for each one.

PROBLEMS	IDEAS
1 People drop rubbish everywhere.	Put rubbish bins in the woods.
2 People take their dogs into the woods.	Put up a sign 'No Dogs'.
3 People take birds' eggs.	Build boxes for birds.
4 People walk everywhere and destroy the plants.	Make some paths between the trees.
5 Farm animals sometimes go into the woods.	Build a fence.

If we put rubbish bins in the woods, people wouldn't drop rubbish everywhere.

4 How was Stonehenge built?

Read about how they built Stonehenge. Can you complete the text with the correct form of the passive?

Stonehenge is a group of enormous stones in the south of Britain. The stones all stand in a circle. Archaeologists think that work 1 ___was started___ (start) on Stonehenge about 5,000 years ago. They think that, first, one large stone 2 _____ (place) in the centre of a circle and then many wooden posts 3 _____ (put) into the ground around it. Later, many different kinds and sizes of stones 4 _____ (bring) from other parts of the country. Eighty-two huge bluestones 5 _____ (transport) from South Wales by boats.

Other stones, weighing more than 50 tonnes, 6 _____ (pull) 30 kilometres across the land on carts. The stones 7 _____ (shape) with stone tools and then levers 8 _____ (use) for the first time to lift the stones into position.

Why did they do it? No one is sure. Some archaeologists say that it 9 _____ (make) as a calendar so that the local people would know when to plant their crops. Other historians say that it 10 _____ (design) as a religious temple. Stonehenge is another of history's mysteries.

🔊 Listen and check your answers.

A vocabulary map (6)
Wonders of the world

Write these words in the correct area of the vocabulary map. (Some words can go in two or more areas.) You can also add the meanings in your language (in the bottom half of each box). Can you add any more words that you know or any more areas to the map?

abandoned city building cool create damage destroy
enormous erupt fantastic glacier guard impressive
interesting isolated maintain monument move apart pour
preserve protect pull apart pyramid renovate repair
respect restore rock formation romantic volcano

TYPES OF FAMOUS PLACES

WONDERS OF THE WORLD

USEFUL VERBS TO TALK ABOUT THE MOVEMENT OF THE EARTH

USEFUL VERBS TO TALK ABOUT FAMOUS PLACES

ADJECTIVES TO DESCRIBE WONDERS OF THE WORLD

Help yourself with …

Here are some ideas to help you help yourself.

Help yourself with spelling

1 Look, cover, write, check

Look at a word,
cover it up,
write it down,
check it.

2 Your mistakes

Look at your work. Make a list of your spelling
mistakes. Put your mistakes into groups.

Double letters:	putting, beginning
	travelling
No 'e':	driving, closing, leaving
ea :	disappear, disease, steal
ee :	need, agree, screen

Help yourself with grammar

3 Cut and mix

Copy some sentences.

Cut the sentences into three parts:
subject, verb, object.
Mix them up.
Make some new sentences.

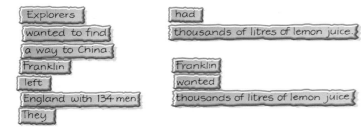

4 Write your own sentences

Copy a sentence.

Describe it.
Write five similar sentences.

PAST SIMPLE	+WHILE	+PAST CONTINUOUS
I saw an accident	while	I was walking in the town.
I did my homework	while	my brother was playing football.

5 Change some sentences

Copy a sentence.

Make it negative or positive.
Make it into a question.
Put it in the past, present or future.

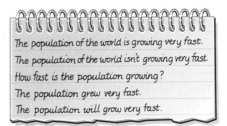

The population of the world is growing very fast.
The population of the world isn't growing very fast.
How fast is the population growing?
The population grew very fast.
The population will grow very fast.

Help yourself with vocabulary

6 Make a word bag

Write some words on pieces of card.
Write the meaning on the other side.
Put the cards in a bag. Take
one out and test yourself.

7 Make a jigsaw

Copy a paragraph from your book. Cut out some
words. Mix them up. Put the words in the right place.

The [   ] of the world
is growing very fast. In the
last 40 years, it has [   ]
By the year 2200, it will
be about 10,000 [   ]
Our [   ] will be much
bigger. There will be [   ]
factories and more roads.
We will [   ] more water
and more natural [   ]

population doubled million
cities more need resources

8 Make a crossword

Make a list of new words. Make a crossword with
them. Write the meaning in your language beside each
word.

```
H
Y               G
D I S A P P E A R
R     A         N
O     M     L E A D
G     P   F O R C E
E     L         A
N     E         T
                E X P L O D E
```

Help yourself with a dictionary

9 Look at your dictionary

A good dictionary has a lot of information. Check
your dictionary against this list. Tick (✓) the box.

List of irregular verbs ☐

Useful phrases ☐

Pronunciation guide ☐

List of abbreviations ☐

Grammar guide ☐

Weights and measures ☐

Other things ☐

10 Information about a word

A good dictionary can tell you a lot about a word.
Look at a word – for example 'see'. Check your
dictionary with these questions.

Does it tell you

– how to say the word? (/siː/) ☐

– what type of word it is? (a verb) ☐

– the past forms? (saw, seen) ☐

– the different meanings? ☐

Does it give you some examples? ☐

11 Check it!

If you have a bilingual dictionary, you can check the
meaning twice.

> Find a word in your language and find the meaning in
> English. Now find the English word in the other half of the
> dictionary. Is the translation the same?

Help yourself with fluency

12 Phrases in a bag

Write some phrases on some cards.
Write them in your language
on the other side. Put the cards
in a bag. Take one out and test
yourself.

What are you up to?

13 Talk to yourself!

Record some questions on a cassette. Play the cassette
and talk to yourself!

Hello, how are you today?

14 Have a conversation

Put two chairs near each other. Sit on one chair and
ask a question. Change chairs and answer your
question. Have a conversation! You can change your
coat or hat as you speak.

What have you done today?

Well, I've done all my homework.
What about you?

Language summaries

Units 1 and 2

SPECIAL VERBS: VERBS + '-ING'

Some verbs in English are 'special'. The verb *after* them usually has '–ing' at the end. Most of these verbs are about likes and dislikes:

> like   hate   love   don't mind
> dislike   enjoy
> I like cook**ing**.

or about starting and stopping:

> start   stop   continue   finish   begin
> I **start**ed learn**ing** English one year ago.

ADVERBS

Adverbs *describe* the verb. They say *how* somebody or something did something. They usually come *after* the verb. For most adverbs, you add '-ly' to the adjective.

> slow → slowly: Please drive slowly
> near the school.

If the adjective has -y at the end, the adverb ends with '-ily'.

> easy → easily: I did that homework easily.

Some adverbs are different!

> good → well   fast → fast   hard → hard
> She studied hard for many years so now she speaks Spanish very well. She can speak very fast.

PAST SIMPLE

You use the Past simple to talk about something at a certain time in the past. For example, yesterday, last night, in 1993 and 4,000 years ago.

> The past of 'be' is 'was' and 'were'.
> I was at school yesterday but David and Julie weren't there.

Some verbs are regular. They all have '-ed' on the end. The ending is the same for all the personal pronouns.

> I walked to the park yesterday and played tennis for three hours.

Some verbs are irregular – they do not use '-ed'. They make the past form in different ways. (Look at the list of irregular verbs in the Student's Book.) The form is the same for all the pronouns.

> go → went We went on holiday to France last year.
> make → made My brother made a cake last week.
> see → saw I saw Peter last Thursday.
> have → had They had a lot of homework last night.

Regular and irregular verbs use 'did' to make questions and negatives.

> – Did you watch the news on TV last night?
> – No, I didn't. I didn't finish my homework until very late.
> – What homework did you do?

'GOING TO'

You can use 'going' to talk about plans for the future.

> We're going to have a picnic on Sunday.

You can also use 'going to' to talk about things that are certain to happen.

> Look at the sky. It's going to rain!

'HAVE TO'

You can use 'have to' to say it is necessary to do something.

> I have to work from 9 am to 5 pm.
> He has to do his homework tonight.

You make the negative with 'doesn't/don't'. In the past, you use 'had to' or 'didn't have to'.

> I don't have to go to school on Saturdays. Last year, I had to go on Saturday mornings but I didn't have to do so much homework.

'ENOUGH'

'Enough' means that there is the right quantity. 'Not enough' means there is less than you want or need. 'Enough' goes *before* a noun and *after* an adjective or a verb.

> There is enough food here for 100 people!
> He hasn't got enough money to buy a car. He doesn't earn enough.

Theme A

'ANYBODY, ANYTHING, ANY...'

You can use 'any' in positive sentences to mean 'not a particular person/thing/place'.

> Anybody can learn English.
> You can sit anywhere you want.

PAST CONTINUOUS

You use the Past continuous to describe or ask about the background for another action. Notice the form.

> 'was/were' + verb + '-ing'
> They found the graves when they were searching Devon Island.
> What were the sailors doing when they saw Franklin's ships?

You can also say 'while' instead of 'when' for the background action.

> Franklin and his men died while they were looking for a route through the Arctic.

ZERO CONDITIONAL/CAUSE AND EFFECT

You can use 'if' (for things that can happen) or 'when' (for definite things) to talk about cause and effect. Notice that you use the Present simple in both parts of the sentence.

> If you don't go to school, you don't learn anything.
> When it rains, the sky becomes darker.

MODALS: 'SHOULD, MIGHT, NEED, MUST'

Modal verbs add to the meaning of a sentence. Notice that you use an infinitive after 'should', 'might' and 'must', but an infinitive with 'to' after 'need'.

> 'should' = an obligation to do something. I should go to bed.
> 'might' = a possibility. I might go to bed after the film.
> 'need' = it is necessary. I need to go to bed. I'm very tired.
> 'must' = have to. I must go to bed. I'm falling asleep.

Be careful with 'must'. The opposite is *not* 'mustn't'. It is 'don't have to'.

> I must go to school tomorrow, but I don't have to go on Friday.

Theme B

PRESENT PERFECT

You can use the Present perfect to talk about a past action that has a result now.

> I have broken my leg. I can't walk.
> I have seen that film, so I know what it is about.

You can also use the Present perfect to talk about an action in 'now' time (today, this morning (when it is still morning), this year, etc.).

> I have done a lot of work today.
> I have spent too much money this week.

Notice that if you say a definite past time, you have to use the Past simple.

> I have seen that film. I saw it last week.

You make the Present perfect with 'has/have' + a past participle. *Regular* past participles end in '-ed'. See the list of irregular verbs in your Student's Book for *irregular* verbs.

> I have seen that film.
> He/she/it has worked very hard.
> You have done a lot today.
> We have visited a lot of places.
> They have spent a lot of money.
> You have walked 30 km today.

FUTURE SIMPLE

You can use the Future simple with 'will' to talk about the future, especially predictions.

> By the year 2200, the world population will be 10,000 million.

(You can also use 'will' for offers. See page 95.)

You can use 'will' for all persons. Notice the form: 'will' + infinitive. The short form is ''ll', and 'won't' is the negative short form.

> I'll (will) see him next week. I won't see him today.
> You'll be tired tomorrow. You won't sleep enough.
> She'll arrive late today. She won't leave on time.
> We'll see you tomorrow. We won't see you tonight.
> You'll like that film. You won't like this film.
> They'll come at 6.00 pm. They won't stay long.

Some people also say 'shall' with 'I' and 'we':

> I shall know the results of my test tomorrow.
> We shall see you next month.

For questions, you normally use 'shall' with 'I' and 'we':

> Shall I see you at the party?
> Will you come to the party?
> Will he/she/it work?
> Shall we come at six o'clock?
> Will you see John tonight?
> Will they eat with us?

Note: you can also use the Present continuous and 'going to' for the future. You can use the Present continuous for plans, especially for a definite time:

> I'm playing football tomorrow afternoon.
> I'm working on Thursday.

See 'going to' in the summary for Units 1 and 2.

FIRST CONDITIONAL

You can use the 'if' + 'will' form to talk about possible future cause and effect.

> If my football team wins this game, they will win the cup.
> If you are in the garden, you won't hear the telephone.

Theme C

PAST PERFECT

You can use the Past perfect to talk about an action that comes before another action in the past.

> When I came home last night I found that Steve had cooked the dinner.

You can also use the Past perfect to talk about a past action with a past result.

> He had broken his leg so he came to school by car.

GERUNDS

Prepositions are words like 'of, in, at, about, for, with, by, up, down, from'. If you use a *verb after a preposition*, you usually have to use the '-ing' form.

> Instead of using a pen, you can use a computer.
> Are you interested in learning about computers?
> The only way you can learn is by using a computer.

If you want to use a *verb as a noun* you usually have to use the '-ing' form also.

> Swimming is very good for you.
> Reading English magazines is a good way to improve your English.

Theme D

'USED TO'

You can use 'used to' to talk about things that happened regularly in the past and that don't happen now. You can use 'used to' with all pronouns ('I, you, he/she/it, we, you, they').

> We used to play football at school but now we play in the park.
>
> I used to live in a big city. Now I live in a small town.

You make questions with 'did' and negatives with 'didn't'.

> Where did you use to live?
>
> Did you use to have long hair?
>
> I didn't use to eat lunch at school. Now I eat there every day.
>
> She didn't use to be a teacher. She used to be a doctor.

You can use 'never' to make a negative sentence.

> I never used to like Maths. Now I think it's great!
>
> She never used to go swimming. Now she swims every day.

RELATIVE CLAUSES

A relative clause gives details about the subject of a sentence. You can use 'that', 'which' and 'who' in relative clauses. You use 'who' with people:

> The people who live next door play loud music every night.
> The teacher who taught us last year is in another school now.

and 'which' for things:

> The book which I left on the bus is very expensive.

You can often use 'that' instead of 'which' or 'who'.

> The people that came to school yesterday were building a new wall.
>
> The book that she posted hasn't arrived yet.

You can often find relative clauses in definitions:

> A dictionary is a book which explains the meanings of words.
>
> An archaeologist is a person who digs up things from the past.

Theme E

QUESTION TAGS

A question tag is two words – a verb and a pronoun. You can use question tags at the end of a sentence when you are speaking (not usually when you are writing). You can use them in two ways. The melody (up or down) is important:

> Her name is Mary, isn't it? (I am sure that's Mary, agree with me.)

> Her name is Mary, isn't it? (I think that's Mary, correct me if I am wrong.)

Be careful! Question tags change with the main verb in the sentence. If the sentence is positive, the question tag is negative; if the sentence is negative, the question tag is positive. Look:

> – +
> They aren't from Italy, are they?
> + –
> He lives in that house, doesn't he?

The form of the question tag changes, too. With, 'be', 'can', 'have' and many modal verbs, you repeat the verb in the tag.

> It(s) a beautiful day, (isn't)it?
>
> He(can't) drive, (can) he?
>
> This train(will) arrive at 7.00 pm, (won't) it?

With all other verbs, you have to use 'do/does/did'.

That car (looks) dangerous, (doesn't) it?

They (live) in Rome, (don't) they?

You (came) home very late last night, (didn't) you?

With 'Let's' the question tag is 'shall we':

Let's go to the cinema tonight, shall we?

PRESENT PASSIVE

You can use the passive voice in English if you want to talk about:

a an action that is more important than who does it:

Thousands of cars are stolen every day.

b a process:

The milk is heated and then it is cooled very quickly.

c a rule:

Eating is not permitted in the library.

You make the Present passive with 'be' + the past participle. (See the list of irregular verbs in your Student's Book.)

Subject + present of 'be' + past participle
The letters are collected at 4 pm.

Theme F

SECOND CONDITIONAL

You can use the second conditional when you want to talk about things that are not real now. They can be very improbable:

If we had wings we would live in trees.

Or a little bit improbable:

If I went to the moon I would take lots of photographs.

Or possible:

If my friends lived next door we would walk to school together.

Notice the form:

'if' + Past simple, 'would' + infinitive
If she posted the letter today it would arrive next week.

You can also reverse the clauses:

The letter would arrive next week, if she posted it today.

'UNLESS'

You can use 'unless' to mean 'if I/you/he (etc.) don't'.

Unless we go now, we will miss the bus.
= If we don't go now, we will miss the bus.
I'll tell him tomorrow, unless you see him first.
= I'll tell him tomorrow, if you don't see him first.

Notice that 'unless' is used like the first conditional. (See Grammar summary for Theme B.)

PAST PASSIVE

The Past passive is used in the same way as the Present passive (see the summary for Theme E), but to talk about the past:

a an action that was more important than who did it.

The first car was made in 1909.

b a process:

Many years ago, ice was collected in Norway, then it was put on boats and taken to England where it was used in food and drink for rich people.

c a rule:

In the past, women were not allowed to vote.

You make the Past passive with 'be' + the past participle. (See the list of irregular verbs in your Student's Book.)

Subject + past of 'be' + past participle
This house was built in 1575.
These tools were made 5,000 years ago.

You can often use the Past passive when you don't know who did something, or you don't want to say.

These cave paintings were hidden behind a rock.
The window was broken last night.

ARGUING A POINT

You can say what you think:

I think you should …   You have to …

You should …   I'm sure …

You can react to what somebody says like this:

That doesn't matter.
I don't think so.
It's the principle that's important.
That's not the point.
Why should I …?

CHECKING

You can use a question tag to check if something is correct (see Grammar summary for Theme E):

This is your book, isn't it?

You can also use other phrases:

Is that right?   Do you mean …?   You mean …?

CLASSROOM PHRASES

You can ask for help in your English lessons:

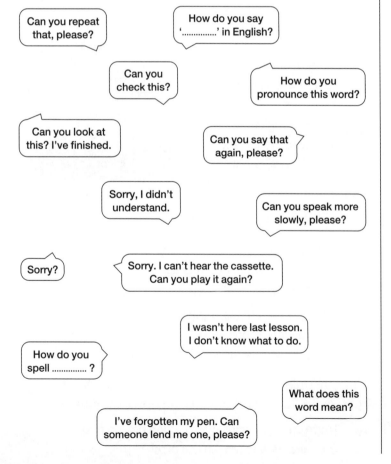

Can you repeat that, please?

How do you say '..............' in English?

Can you check this?

How do you pronounce this word?

Can you look at this? I've finished.

Can you say that again, please?

Sorry, I didn't understand.

Can you speak more slowly, please?

Sorry?

Sorry. I can't hear the cassette. Can you play it again?

I wasn't here last lesson. I don't know what to do.

How do you spell .... ?

I've forgotten my pen. Can someone lend me one, please?

What does this word mean?

DESCRIBING AN ACTION

You can describe an action using an adverb (see the Grammar summary for Units 1 and 2):

He does all his work very carefully.

You can use the Past continuous to describe what was happening at the same time as a past action (see the Grammar summary for Theme A):

I was sleeping when I heard a noise downstairs.

You can use a gerund when the action is the subject of a sentence (see the Grammar summary for Theme C):

Smoking is bad for you.

You can use a modal to describe how important or likely an action is (see the Grammar summary for Theme A):

I might go to the town centre tomorrow because I need to buy some things. I should get a new bag for school and I must buy a new pen.

You can talk about actions that happened regularly in the past with 'used to' (see the Grammar summary for Theme D):

Thousands of years ago, people used to live in caves. They used to hunt for their food.

DESCRIBING CAUSE AND EFFECT

You can use a zero conditional to talk about things that always happen if (or when) you do something (see the Grammar summary for Theme A):

If you cut yourself, blood comes out.
When the winter comes, many birds fly south.

You can use a first conditional to talk about possible future events (see the Grammar summary for Theme B):

If the ice melts, the sea level will rise.

You can use a second conditional to talk about improbable or unlikely future events (see the Grammar summary for Theme F):

If I met the President, I would ask her to stop all wars.

You can use the Present perfect to talk about the present result of a past action (see the Grammar summary for Theme B):

> I have lost my pen. I can't do my homework!

In the same way, you can use the Past perfect to talk about the past result of a past action (see the Grammar summary for Theme C):

> I had forgotten my money so I couldn't buy a drink.

DESCRIBING OBJECTS

You can describe objects in different ways:

> It's got …
> The material is …
> There's … on the bottom/top/side.
> It's beautiful.

EXPLAINING A PROCESS

You can explain a process clearly if you use words like 'First, …'. and 'Next, …' to explain the sequence:

> **Printing a book**
> First, they type all the text into a computer. Next, they print it out and check it carefully. Then, they divide it into pages. When they have done that, they ask artists to draw the pictures. Finally, they put the text and the pictures together and make special plates for the printing press.

GIVING EXTRA DETAILS

You can use relative clauses to say more about somebody or something, or to be clear what you mean (see the Grammar summary for Theme D):

> The dog that bit me lives next door.
> People who are colour blind cannot see red or green well.

INVITING AND SUGGESTING

You can invite someone to do something or go somewhere. You can also suggest what you can do.

> Why don't you come with me?
> Why don't we meet at my house?
> Would you like to come?
> Shall I tell …?
> Let's meet at around five, shall we?
> See you later.

You can use 'will' to offer to do something:

> I'll carry that heavy bag for you.
> I'll open the window.

You can use 'would' to offer someone something:

> Would you like a drink of orange?
> Would you like to come to my party?

OFFERS

See Inviting and suggesting.

OPINIONS

You can express your opinions like this:

> I think it's a great idea.
> I don't think it's such a good idea.
> Why should Bill Jones organise a team only for boys?
> Things used to be like that, but things are different now.

You can ask someone about their opinions like this:

> What do you think?
> What do you think about …?
> What's your opinion?
> Do you really think …?

You can react to and criticise an idea in many ways. For example, you can repeat what the person has said but in a different way.

> – I'm going to fast for 24 hours.
> – You mean you're not going to eat for 24 hours!

PREDICTING

You use the Future simple to talk about future predictions (see the Grammar summary for Theme B):

> I think many people will live underground in the year 2200. We will all work at home. Nobody will work in factories because robots will do everything.

RESPONSIBILITY AND FAIRNESS

You can say if you think someone is responsible for something, or you aren't responsible, and argue your point:

> It is your responsibility.
> It's your fault.
> You have to …
> It's not fair.
> It's not my fault. I didn't do it.
> That's not the point.
> It's none of your business.

Acknowledgements

The authors and publishers are grateful to the following illustrators and photographic sources:

Illustrators: Gerry Ball: pp. 18, 19*t*, 50*t*; James Bartholomew: pp. 10*t*, 28, 57; Robert Calow: pp. 5, 7*t*, 14, 19 *b*, 26, 35, 41, 42, 46*t*, 52, 53, 72*br*, 74, 77, 89*b*; Lee Ebrell: pp. 80, 81; Hilary Evans: handwritten items; Gecko Ltd: maps on pp. 8 and 58; Phil Healey: pp. 55, 65*t*; Steve Lach: pp. 7*b*, 24*t*, 25, 27*t*, 37*t*, 45, 56, 88, 89*t*, 90, 91, 92, 93, 94; Sally Launder: pp. 12, 15, 21, 24*b*, 27*b*, 33*b*, 37*b*, 40*b*, 43, 50*b*, 62, 63, 65*b*, 66, 72 tl, 75, 76*t*, 79*t*, 82, 83; David Mitcheson: pp. 10*b*, 11, 38, 39, 40*t*, 46*b*, 76*b*, 78–79; James Sneddon: all DTP illustrations and graphics; John Storey: pp. 22, 32, 33*t*, 34, 47, 60, 73, 85, 86.

Photographic sources: Barnaby's Picture Library/BOAC: p. 36(b), Barnaby's/Bea Hunn: p. 16(a), Barnaby's/West Air: p. 79; Camera Press Limited/Lennox Smillie: p. 28; Sue Cunningham Photographic: p. 36(e); Mary Evans Picture Library: pp. 21, 85; Getty Images: p. 48, Getty Images/James Martin: p. 84*br*, Getty Images/Greg Pease: p. 16(e), Getty Images/Michael Scott: p. 84*tr*; Richard Greenhill: p. 49*t*; Robert Harding Picture Library: p. 13*b*, R. Harris/Robert Harding Picture Library: p. 8, J.H.C. Wilson/Robert Harding Picture Library: p. 36(c); Images Colour Library: pp. 70, 84*tl*, 84*bl*; Peter Arkell/Impact Photos: p. 49*b*; Nigel Luckhurst: p. 27; Sam Abell/National Geographic Image Collection: p. 57; Andrew Hasson/The Observer: p. 13*t*; Pictor International: p. 16(b); Popperfoto: p. 11*r*; Redferns/William Gottlieb: p. 36(d); Spectrum Colour Library: p. 16(d), Spectrum/D. & J. Heaton: p. 9; T. Matsumoto/Sygma: p. 25; Telegraph Colour Library/Benelux Press: p. 36(a), Telegraph/Planet Earth/David A. Ponton: p. 16(c); Topham Picturepoint: p. 11*l*.

t = top *b* = bottom *l* = left *r* = right

Picture research by Sandie Huskinson-Rolfe of PHOTOSEEKERS.

Cover design by Dunne & Scully based on an illustration by Felicity Roma Bowers.

Sound recordings by Martin Williamson, Prolingua Productions at Studio AVP.

Freelance editorial work by Helena Gomm.

Design and production by Gecko Ltd., Bicester, Oxon.